The Circle, Cubed

The Circle, Cubed

Erecting the Temple in Four Dimensions

Kaatryn MacMorgan-Douglas

COVENSTEAD PRESS   BUFFALO, NEW YORK

© 2008, Kaatryn MacMorgan-Douglas
All Rights Reserved
ISBN: 978-0-6151-9070-9

Permission is freely granted for the liturgical use of any rituals given in this book; however, they *may not* be republished, placed on websites or otherwise used in any manner without the explicit consent of the author.

This book is not available as a download. If you have received a digital copy it was stolen. There are no "digital resale rights" available for this work. In other words, it may not be added to CD-Rom collections, sold as a digital copy by auction or otherwise abused. Please respect our community's authors.

For more information: http://www.covensteadpress.com

Please note that the three pieces of bonus material have their own copyrights. The Compass Rose and Heraldic Circle is © 2007 Kaatryn MacMorgan-Douglas, and the Elemental Visualizations and similar material from *All One Wicca* are used with permission and are ©1997, 2001 and 2007. For the proper way to attribute them, please email the author, or list them as reprinted in "The Circle, Cubed," ©2008 Kaatryn MacMorgan-Douglas.

This work is dedicated to all of my teachers; teachers of life, magic, Wicca, languages, sciences, rhetoric and culture.

There is no greater title to be earned than that of teacher.

Introduction:

There are five dimensions to erecting the temple in Wicca, five aspects of the rite that transcend sect or tradition, coven membership or solitary practice, beginners and elders. These dimensions are the spiritual, the physical, the mental, the traditional and the energetic. This book covers four of the dimensions alone.

The fifth dimension, the energetic dimension, is not something you can learn online or through a book. It is ideally something you experience with another and learn to replicate with practice. It can be mastered without the intervention of another soul nonetheless, but no words on paper can train you to do it. This is one reason why I disagree with online schools that do not require offline practice, visualization and meditation as a regular part of their lesson sets.

I am avoiding the energetic dimension because it would do you a disservice to claim my exercises or experiences could give it to you in this context. What I can say is that practice of these other four aspects will often cause you to sense the fifth. Pursue that sense, experiment with it, and you will be rewarded with the knowledge of the fifth in time.

A faster form of training can be found by meeting other Wiccans and erecting the temple together, but I believe the sanctity of an individual's energy is such that one should be wary of mixing energies freely with strangers. Those of us who are sensitive to the pattern and flow of others can find our own inner bright light dimmed by proximity to many types of people. Once your energy, regardless of what you call it or how you define it, leaves the boundary of the personal, it mingles with the extrapersonal, and it is no longer yours alone; mix carefully.

Those familiar with my other works know that I don't hold much truck with doing things with no reason, and as a result a lot of what you may find definitive to a circle or erecting the temple rite within your tradition or personal practice may be left out, or treated critically herein. This is not out of malice or anger, but because I intend to present a definitive discussion of erecting the temple rites and that includes discussing both the techniques and their basis.

As always, I encourage—no, *beg*—you to take nothing I present here as fact. Do the research yourself, ask your elders, consult your traditions, visit the library and practice every technique you can get your hands on. I am not a guru, a saint, the queen of the witches, a goddess or anything but a simple human being, and that simple human being is as flawed as any other. Trust no author merely because they are an author. Trust people only because you have done the research and found it worthy of your trust. Facts, not names or titles, are worth trusting.

As with my past several works, this book is not about the tradition of Wicca I practice–Universal Eclectic Wicca. This book is for Wiccans of all traditions including UEW. That being said, I encourage those solitary practitioners and eclectic coven members who do not have a tradition to seek one out, whether it be UEW or not. In my experience, the best traditions will accept solitaries freely and are themselves eclectic. Learning within a tradition helps to give you a scaffold of non-contradictory belief and practice from which you can build the Wicca your heart and your gods desire you to practice.

Some will say that they cannot join a tradition because they don't want to blindly follow a leader or a book. I say to those who claim this that you are *already* blindly following someone—experience a decent tradition and you will see it's anything but blind following. I am asked often how I learned so very much and without a doubt having elders and friends to learn from and explore topics with is why my knowledge base is broad. Do not limit yourself to practice inside a tiny box for fear of being trapped inside with a big one. You can always change or leave traditions as your experiences require.

While this book is not presented as an advanced level work, and, indeed, literacy in the temple rites should be within any good Wiccan's first-year learning goals, there are some rites herein that assume you know how to do various parts of the ritual. I have tried to include a broad mix of rituals, so it is inevitable that experienced Wiccans may find the practice sections overly simplistic and that newcomers to Wicca may find the language of some of the advanced rites beyond their ken. While I genuinely believe there is nothing in here beyond a first-year understanding, it may be necessary for some readers to seek information in other sources.

I would be lying, however, if I did not say that I think my own students, and the students in UEW they have taught, should find nothing herein remotely difficult to grasp. Most of the instances where I have not clarified the action within a rite to the point of absurdity can be performed even by a beginner by assuming that they know what they are doing.

In the sole rite within I consider truly advanced (excluding the bonus materials) two of my lovely readers and newcomers to Wicca had trouble with the line "call to mind the triumph of spirit over will," I asked both to meditate on the concept and they had no trouble finding the right mindspace and mental exercise required. With that instance in mind, I really do think there is nothing herein beyond the level of a beginner, provided the beginner is willing to work through those things they consider difficult.

With that in mind, however, many of the rites herein aren't for everyone…it is unimportant, for example, if you are a solitary practitioner, to have complete literacy in every group rite herein, although the reverse is not nearly as true.

While learning the canonical temple rite of your tradition is important to any student, usually perfecting your own temple rite is a big step towards self-sufficiency and mastery in Wicca. Consider this book a *reference* for this vital first-year task, a guide to crafting your unique temple rite. Use the sample rituals to help yourself become familiar with what the temple really does and then craft your own body of work based on that knowledge.

As I say to my students, make the temple rite your own, with a strong foundation in the five essential dimensions. Learn what the rite is doing at the level of the spiritual, the physical, the mental, the traditional and the energetic and then make your unique rite do the same thing.

Table of Contents

Introduction: i
Table of Contents v
Chapter One: What is Erecting the Temple? 1
Chapter Two: Temples of Spirit 6
Chapter Three: Physical Temples 13
Chapter Four: Temples of the Mind 24
Chapter Five: Temples of Tradition 31
Chapter Six: Holistic Temples 35
Chapter Seven: Minimalist Temples 43
Chapter Eight: Debates in Temple Construction 47
Chapter Nine: Temples for Formal Worship 51
Chapter Ten: Closing the Temple 63
Chapter Eleven: When to not use the Temple 65
General Purification Techniques 67
General Mental Preparedness Techniques 69
Four Additional Erecting the Temple Rites 70
Glossary 77
Introduction to Bonus Material 79
Bonus Material-Ritual of the Compass Rose 81
Bonus Material-The Elemental Visualizations 109
Bonus Material-The Heraldic Circle 118
Afterword: I know how to do this, now what? 126
Index 128

Chapter One: What is Erecting the Temple?

Erecting the temple, which is often called casting the circle, is a rite within the Wiccan religion. In traditional Wiccan practice a rite is a ritual fragment, a portion of a ritual that (combined with other rites) makes up a complete celebratory practice. For example, a Full Moon celebration could include the erecting the temple rite, a shared feast rite (often called cakes and ale), a celebratory lunar rite and a clearing the temple or closing the circle rite. The actual celebration itself may be referred to as a Full Moon rite or Full Moon ritual, but the term implies the fragment, not the whole of the celebration.

Erecting the temple is the beginning of the general liturgical practice in a Wiccan holy ritual. Its most basic form, found in the publicly accessible Gardnerian Book of Shadows[1], consists of drawing or marking a line on the boundary of the circle,[2] exhorting various entities, consecrating some water and salt, sprinkling it around the circle, lighting some candles then walking around the circle repeatedly as dictated by tradition. This creates a space in which the Wiccan ritual is performed, sort of like building a church or putting up a tent.

The circle is reminiscent of King Arthur's Round Table–all who stand in it are at an equal place, none higher or lower than any other. Like Arthur's table, this equity is usually an illusion, with those closest to the one with the highest rank deemed of a higher rank than those furthest, but the reminder is there nonetheless– there is no one truly higher or lower in the circle, all are equal in the view of the gods.

Gardner conflated the blessing of the meeting found in most fraternal organizations with the magical circles of Dee and other ceremonial magicians, and this created an imperfection in the rite. Gardner's circle is a preparation of a space for communion with the

---

[1] Available at http://www.sacred-texts.com/pag/gbos/index.htm
[2] Gardner used a 9ft circumference. I believe that if one is to be accurate based on Gardner's *intent*, not his actual writing, this should be twice that, as his number assuredly comes from Mather's version of the *Clavicula Salomonis* and was misunderstood by Gardner.

divine, and ceremonial magic's circle keeps something in, or keeps something out. This flaw has led to a constant tweaking in the circle rite by those that have followed Gardner[3], and this is one reason why we see a more elaborate version eight years later in the public Gardnerian Book of Shadows with a rudimentary Charge of The Goddess and Drawing Down the Moon rite. By the mid-1980s, most versions encompassed salt and water, candles at four compass points, incense, wine, oil, an offering and much more, making the erecting the temple rite sometimes take nearly twice as long as the ritual it contains.

Each of the revisions of the erecting the temple rite has added new elements, often from ceremonial magic but occasionally from Christianity or other forms of Abrahamic religion, to the point where those familiar with the forms being plundered to enhance the circle often feel the urge to rip their hair out in frustration as newcomers throw in various terms and practices without even a rudimentary understanding of those terms and dictate that they are both essential to Wicca and have been always practiced by Wiccans.

Gardner himself said "The only circle that matters is the one drawn before every ceremony with either a duly consecrated Magic Sword or an Athamé.[4]" The common belief by many is that he was distinguishing this circle from those drawn in physical form, but as he called the rite in question a circle it stands to reason that he was trying to convey that the energetic circle, not the rite around it, was of importance.

I will therefore define the circle or temple in this work not as a magical circle but instead something closer to the starting ritual of a fraternal organization. The erecting the temple rite will instead be herein understood as preparing the way for the worship of the gods and the journey within. The phrase "preparing the way" should make your ears perk up, and if you are in any way unsure about a temple Rite, ask if it is "preparing the way." If the rite is not preparing the way, it is missing its key function.

---

[3] Myself included. My *Ritual of the Compass Rose* pretty much rewrote it from scratch.
[4] http://www.sacred-texts.com/pag/gbos/gbos00.htm

If we define the rite as preparing the way, we can evaluate the functionality of the rite based on how well it prepares the way in each of the four dimensions this book covers. Does the rite prepare the way in a spiritual, physical, mental, and traditional manner, or does it leave out one or more of these aspects?

An erecting the temple rite prepares the way in a spiritual manner by making the place where the rite is going to be performed in accordance with the gods, the ancestors and other things of spirit. It makes certain that the area a ritual is going to occur in is right with the divine in all ways. If, for example, you were to use an otherwise perfectly functional erecting the temple rite in land sacrosanct to the gods or ancestors, you could not prepare the way spiritually because sacrosanct land is literally set aside, lands that are to be left alone. The spiritual dimension, then, involves rightness with the gods and other non-physical or extra-physical beings, not merely calling them or inviting them, but by respecting them.

More tangible by far are the physical aspects of the temple, which can range from drawing a circle on the ground or placing candles to creating a specifically targeted ritual structure, out of "spirit or stone[5]," or even lumber. Much of the overly complex ritual out there is focused upon this aspect of the rite, but it's not something one should feel free to discard without reason. The physical marking out of the ritual creates a place aside, a place that is said to be of this world and not of this world. It is a place where the human mind and body can easily understand where it is supposed to be, and that is what the physical dimension of the circle is, an easily understandable space that is prepared to hold the acts of worship or celebration.

As with much of the rest of universe, the physical begets the mental. The spiritual prepares the way by making it right with the sacred ones of our universe, the physical prepares the way by marking a space in the universe and the mental prepares the way by making a direct change in our brain-space, within the boundaries of our mind. It is this mental dimension that UEW focuses upon with its elemental states visualizations, the change within the self that prepares the way for the mental aspects of ritual, the changes within

---

[5] From the Silver Chalice Ordains.

the self that causes knowledge of will, to paraphrase a Thelemic worldview.

Each of these dimensions of the rite causes a strengthening in its tangibility. The spiritual reverberates with the gods, the physical with space and the mental with the will. The traditional dimension of a temple rite strengthens it by reverberating with the practices you and others of similar teachings to yours have done throughout time and space. In other words, the traditional dimension can be understood as using techniques the universe as a whole has experienced in the past and in the future. The difference between a rite or ritual fragment used the first time and a rite or ritual fragment used repeatedly is like the difference between a well-used tool and a brand new one, both may work, but one generally possesses finesse and other ineffable concepts that a person must experience to understand. Thus distinct phraseology, the use of sacred language or tools, and the use of well-used movements or symbols can each, themselves build upon the reverberations though time/space that the ritual involves.

It is this reason, not vulgar attempts at building up a religion by claiming an ancient history it does not have, which is why Wiccans are often researching the past, although it is most-assuredly a two-edged sword, as not all things can reverberate through space and time in harmony with each other, but that tends to be a knowledge that comes with practice, not from the words of any one author.

Taken with the other dimensions, the traditional dimension helps to build a temple that is tightly constructed, tangible, does exactly what it is designed to do and is understood by all participants within. It is not a magically protective circle[6], as those in the *Clavicula Salomonis* and other medieval grimoires are, although it is possible to structure a temple in that way with a lot of work, a generally pointless exercise.

The erecting the temple rite can come in a multitude of forms fulfilling as little as one or as many of all of our five dimensions. The next four chapters of this book will focus on building a temple in

---

[6] And, indeed, should not be, as the act of building and releasing energy through the structure invoked via an erecting the temple rite does not fit with the purposes thereof. This is generally not understood by those familiar only with temple rites or only with magical circles, however.

one dimension alone, with the hope that practice therein will allow one to complete effective holistic temple rites.

Ideally, this book will leave you with the capacity not only to use any of the rites herein but also to craft new rites which are appropriate for your group or solitary practice. Wicca which does not address the specific needs of the people practicing it is Wicca which has failed as a religion. If it does not work, you need to fix it.

That being said, in my experience there is a new and rising fundamentalism in Wicca. Like all fundamentalist movements, it is rooted in ignorance and fear. One of the myriad false teachings of this movement is the belief that there is only one way to erect the temple appropriate in Wicca and all others are "false Wicca." Modern Wiccan groups claim this belief came from Gardner, and I want to assure people that it really takes a minor amount of research to quickly indicate that this is indeed not the case in the slightest.

Traditionally, Wicca has tailored the rite used to erect the temple to the reasons for the temple's creation. If a major working is to be done, the circle is complex. If a minor working is done, the circle is simple. If the temple involves Hellenic gods, it often focuses upon the classical elements or sacred geometry. If it is for the Celtic deities or even the Roman gods in their aspect as the overarching trade culture deities, the circle might be a triangle. If it is about the changes in a woman's life, it might involve only goddesses, and if it takes place in a pre-ordained space, it may involve the walls of that space.

I will not address the specifics of all the ways to create the temple herein, but I will tell you what those ways are trying to address. From there, the knowledge you learn elsewhere should be enough to construct a functional temple and tweak it until you've manifested an airtight rite that is worthy of your gods.

Chapter Two: Temples of Spirit

Of the four dimensions of circle casting that can be taught via a book, crafting the temple of spirit may be the most nebulous and difficult to grasp, because we literally have no words in English that accurately describe the level of rightness that building a temple of spirit involves. Translations of Zen tend to come close, with the Noble Eightfold Path[7] of Right View, Right Intention, Right Speech, Right Action, Right Livelihood, Right Effort, Right Mindfulness and Right Consciousness. The temple of Spirit is a little bit of all of these, and can be best understood as Right with the Universe.

Rightness with the Universe can essentially be interpreted along the lines of the triarchy of man. We must be right with our animal natures (our base instincts, health, physical well being, etc.), right with our gods and right with our humanity. Of these, rightness with the animal nature is the easiest to grasp, if rather hard to achieve.

While it is acceptable to perform any erecting the temple rite as needed, the ideal rite should occur when the officiate is healthy and his physical needs are met. One should not engage in ritual when hungry, thirsty, tired or otherwise unwell in terms of physical needs. The ritual space must be appropriate to the clothing worn, so going skyclad outside when it is below freezing or wearing heavy and dark velvet robes in the steam of a hot August Eve evening is right out. If you are preparing a rite for many, *their* physical needs should be considered at this point as well as your own–all who enter the temple should be as well as they can be physically, with nothing neglected. This doesn't mean perfect health, but it does mean that if a covener broke his leg, you'd make sure he was in a cast before you let him in a temple.

This also rules out altered states of consciousness when erecting the temple. If you must imbibe or ingest compounds that alter your physical state as part of a ritual of your design, erect the temple before doing so. That being said, as imperfect humans, we often need various medications to be as close to physically fit as possible, so make sure that you haven't missed any medications you need to

---

[7] This is discussed in simple terms online at
http://www.handfulofsand.com/zen/archives/000635.html

approach normal, such as replacement thyroid hormones, serotonin reuptake inhibitors, anti-seizure drugs or appropriate pain killers. Do not cease taking a prescription to erect a temple, as your body is more shocked (and thus "less normal") by stopping and starting drugs than by remaining on them. Rightness with one's animal self, while in many ways similar to other human beings varies a lot from one individual to another, so you have to know yourself and understand your individual needs before even approaching the rite.

Rightness with the gods is less concrete but equally important. We begin to craft Rightness with the gods long before crafting temples of Spirit by being worthy of communion with them. We are generally prepared for this from the moment of birth, but our actions can increase or decrease our relationship with deities. Unfortunately, individual gods often have different requirements, so there is no one formula for being right with all the gods.

As a general formula, one needs to not have any miasma[8] or uncleanliness attached to oneself. Rather than prescribe cleanliness codes, most Wiccans include a form of ritual purification before the ritual, with the assumption that those who've offended the gods or otherwise are problematic aren't going to show up in a space where those who would enter are exhorted to come inside with "Perfect Love and Perfect Trust."

Purification generally takes two forms, the physical form of showering or otherwise cleaning oneself before attending the rite and the more symbolic gestures of lustration. Lustration[9] is the use of incense or burning herbs to make sacred smoke that is passed over or around the individual. It can also be used to refer to anointment, the act of placing a mark of sacred fluid on the body of an individual. Historically, lustration purified the body and anointment purified the soul, so it is typical to see both used in the same ritual. Clothing oneself in ritual purified clothing or removing clothing can also be

---

[8] Probably the most comprehensive discussion of miasma is *Miasma: Pollution and Purification in Early Greek Religion* by Robert Parker, but most will find it a dense and dry study of historic practices.

[9] It is very likely the Classical lustration of sheep also caused some adult sheep ticks to fall off the sheep they would feed on, probably making lustrated sheep healthier. Smoking wool to drive out bugs is a common practice in pre-industrial cultures.

such an act, and some gods expect that the hair will be covered, bound or unbound, depending on the context.

Other ways of becoming right with the gods involve ethics, completing appointed tasks or goals and generally approaching the temple with the respect and honesty expected when you are entering a place that can be understood as a temporary house of the gods. Essentially, within the temple the bonds of guestright are two fold, because you are guests within the house of the gods while they are guests within your rite. Therefore, one should behave as much like a good host and a good guest as possible.

The third set of "Rightness" involved with erecting the temple of spirit is rightness with one's humanity. Humanity is a liminal concept, straddling animal and god, simultaneously both and neither. To prepare one's humanity for entering into communion with the divine and other animals, one must focus on what makes humankind different from animals–the will.

Understanding the concept of the will is probably one of the most important early lessons the Wiccan learns. The will is far more than desire or want, which are relegated to the realm of the animal, and approaches the concept of the will of the gods we see in Abrahamic and Greek Mythology, θέλημα (thelema.[10]) Divine will is something more than human will, having the superior knowledge and abilities of the divine behind it. Human will is when we are most god-like, but our will lacks the powers of the divine.

Human will, then, draws its power from the human equivalent of the power of the divine. This is a poorly defined concept that is actually really easy to comprehend in practice. Put simply, the universe dislikes[11] dissonance, so it attempts to make the strongly believed in reality of a well-formed will come into harmony with the greater reality. *The stronger the will, the stronger the ability to affect change in the greater reality.*

---

[10] There is a common belief in Paganism that θέλημα speaks only to the philosophy of Thelema, and when I write of that, I tend to capitalize it to distinguish it from the idea of divine will itself. The two are interlinked, obviously, but I use the Greek here not to indicate the philosophy but to reference the Attic and the Koine!

[11] I am anthropomorphizing the universe here to make a metaphoric point, not because I advocate belief in the idea of the universe being seen as having traits like those of humans or gods.

Rightness with one's will can be understood as perceiving one's greater path through life and taking steps to move forward in it. It involves seeing yourself as an ideal and taking steps to make the ideal into reality. This is something that has to happen outside the temple before you get to that point, and it's an ongoing process. Meditation, frank inner dialog and transparent inner processing help, but it's not anything a person can do for you.

In addition to one's will, every person who is practicing their religion in accordance with their ancestral traditions or, barring that, respectful of their ancestors, must also practice rightness with one's ancestors. You are the sum of your ancestors as well as something new in the universe and you can't ignore that in the spiritual dimension, even if it covered again in the traditional one. In short, Rightness with the ancestors is fulfilling any blood obligations you have accumulated so that when you erect the temple, you are not divided in your energies between serving the gods and serving others. The ancestors should be kept in mind during the rite, but they should not be invoked unless specifically needed in the rite.

With those things in mind, you should be able to see that the spiritual dimension of erecting the temple is accomplished both in the preparation phase and in the temple itself. In the basic circle recipe, on page 58 of *All One Wicca*, I discussed the following as the bare minimums for erecting the temple, and they are herein refined for our discussion:

- Physical Demarcation of Boundary
- Announcement of intent
- Creation of Spatial/Conceptual Boundaries
- Creation of Metaphysical Boundaries
- Welcoming of Participants
- Welcoming of Gods.
- Announcement of Completion

While the first one is strictly physical, the remaining each have a spiritual component. The announcement of intent is especially powerful as it can be used to make the internal reality transparent both to you and the gods. The fragment below was used to open a large November Eve circle as part of the announcement of intent. This particular circle was cast around the participants, so it also includes the welcoming of the participants. Numbers are placed for further discussion of the individual facets of the fragment:

> We are the ones of the Wicca (1) who have gathered in this place at this time to mark the change of the seasons and turn[12] the wheel of the year(2). We have come together before the eyes of the gods, our ancestors (3) and each other to join with the multitude (4) on this sacred night. All who stand here have been purified(5) with (the elements.) Let none remain for this sacred rite who does not enter in perfect love and perfect trust(6), to mark this time as one people, one mind, and one will.(7)

Part of functioning with will as a human being means that one can speak with authority and make the words more real than they appear on a page. If you haven't been at a ritual like that above, you might not be familiar with the sensation of the air tingling as if the world is waiting in expectation to be told what will occur, or the sense of rush when minds reach an accord.

1 and 7 in the fragment above both mark the people in the circle as one functional unit, expressing that they have a knowledge of the rite that allows them to work as a unit and the associated skills, essentially fulfilling the spiritual dimension of Rightness with mankind. This is stressed again in 6, with the term "Perfect Love and Perfect Trust" reverberating on the traditional dimension as well.

In 2, the fragment hints at divine obligation. The Wiccans in question are there, in part, because of an obligation to themselves and the rest of the world to turn the wheel of the year. I selected a fragment with this ideology to make it clear that Rightness with the Universe involves one's obligations of all sorts, not just seeing that you are prepared with the gods.

In 5, it is noted that the participants have been purified. They are making a space that is appropriate for the presence of the gods and their ancestors to witness them (3) and therefore have had to shuck the debris of the mortal world.

---

[12] There is a significant theological discussion in Wicca as to whether the rituals turn the wheel or mark the turning of the wheel. I tend to fall in the mark the turning camp, but I respect the concept as a metaphor and if accompanied with other actions to stabilize the climate I'm all for energy directed that way.

Lastly, although it mostly reverberates on the traditional dimension, the coven makes it clear to all that are aware of the rite that they are part of many celebrating this night (4) and that they as a unit are interacting with the gods and ancestors to this end. Each of these points adds up to Rightness with the Universe, fulfilling the obligation of the Spiritual temple.

Practice:

Appealing for Help in the Knowledge of one's Self and Obligations:

Additional preparation for the spiritual temple will be covered in each of the following three chapters, to integrate them into the holistic temple in chapter six, but spiritual temples can themselves be erected for personal use as a prayer. The exercise that follows teaches techniques used in the erecting the temple rite. It is absolutely possible for advanced students to skip this or insert an appropriate deity and associated symbolism.

The choice of Apollo for this rite is not accidental, as those who are aware of my personal religions and practices will attest. That I know of, Apollo has never turned away a person sincerely interested in coming to a deeper understanding of their will. Know Thyself is the watchword of Delphi, after all. It's also not a flippant choice, so don't treat this flippantly, don't do it at all if you can't do it in the spirit given.

Please note that there is no claim that this rite is authentic Hellenic Practice, as it assuredly is not.

Begin by showering or otherwise bathing. Don't do a cursory job of it. When you have completed it, dry off and change into a simple robe or other comfortable clean clothing you feel appropriate to the rite. Don't do the rite when you are ill. Most assuredly don't do it if you're in danger of dying any minute. Ideally, do it in a room where no one has died.

Place a tripod of burning coals and laurel to the east. If this is too difficult, you may use contemporary incense. I like labdanum and coriander with laurel for similar rites. Breathe deep several times, then take a prayerful, respectful position. Ideally this is a position that shows respect but does not cause cognitive dissonance. Generally those of us with non-religious backgrounds don't have trouble with kneeling as we don't tend to associate it with church but with respect.

Close your eyes, bow your head and think Apollo. Feel it, mean it. You are a seeker, trying to find yourself. He is a god your ancestors almost assuredly[13] turned to for this very thing. He knows you, and somewhere deep inside you know him.

Remember to breathe. Try to not visualize or force a contact. You don't command gods, at best, you are granted some small attention. You're not seeking to enter a priest position[14] here, just get help from a god that is generally willing to respond to honest seekers. Note I'm not giving you formulae here, please alter appropriately. In my experience, Apollo does not react well to the people who think that something that they can get out of a book is going to make him appear like a servant. Definitely don't LIE.

Look up, speaking to the heavens.

"Apollo the healer, protector of Delphi, leader of the Muses, I am (tell him who you are.)[15] I am trying to come to a better knowledge of myself, my ancestors and my religious beliefs and I ask for any assistance or answers you deem appropriate in coming to that knowledge. I have meditated, sought in books and other media to better know the right way to give honor to all and offense to none. I ask of you whatever help you feel it right to provide, any direction or assistance. If it is your will to help, so be it. If it is not, I accept that as well."

Maintain the appropriate position for a while longer. Allow your mind to be opened to the answers of the universe and the shining one. When appropriate, take the incense outside and allow it to burn away. If you have skill with a musical instrument or your voice you may want to perform to honor him.

If your answers are definitive, I recommend making a votive offering by burying a gold coin and making a donation to a science or youth organization, or both. Such things pay off in the end.

---

[13] If you are even remotely European, you probably had an ancestor or indirect relative make a pilgrimage to Delphi or a similar site. There is evidence of worship of Apollo in North Africa, on the British Isles and in Asia in addition to in the well-known classical sites in Greece and Italy.

[14] If Apollo should will otherwise, your point of view might not count much.

[15] Ex: "I am Maria, daughter of Frank and Esme, a simple computer programmer."

Chapter Three: Physical Temples

Erecting the temple touches many worlds. It touches on the mental world, the inner space no one else can fully grasp. It touches on the spiritual world, where those beings unlike flesh or who have transcended flesh can be encountered without any action on their part. It also touches the physical world, the world you went to sleep in last night and woke up in this morning.

In many ways, the physical temple is the easiest to construct, in that the ability to draw a line with a piece of chalk, drag a sword through the sand or make a line of powder is something all but young children can do easily. Using stones, blocks and rope to mark the boundaries is even easier yet, and perfectly valid in most contexts.

More complicated physically, but less complicated theologically, is the construction of dedicated worship spaces. I personally tend to favor orangeries attached to houses for this, as they can often be ordered with a 21ft diameter, fitting the 18ft Solomanic circle without difficulty, but they are hardly within most people's budgets[16]! Wood gazebos, basement temples and dedicated buildings of all sorts provide a single-use space that remains consecrated by virtue of being set aside.

I'll assume for these purposes that you lack the space or will to create a set-aside physical space and I'll focus instead on the temporary circle most Wiccans use. Traditionally, this is a circle-in-circle format with a tetrad of points, sometimes called the square or the cross in the circle. This "NEWS" circle (upper left) appears in Solomanic magic a lot because it resonates with the Tetragrammaton, the four letter name of the Abrahamic (Jewish, Christian, Muslim) deity. This circle is also conceptualized as a square within a circle (lower left) with the four points representing the same set of directions or letters. This second form is often preferred by Pagans who want to move away from the John Dee concept of the watchtowers or

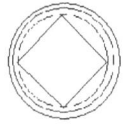

[16] Not within my budget, certainly, although I was fortunate enough to consult for a Pagan installing one, designing what would become the mosaic for the structure.

watchers, but still is generally based on the same set of concepts. John Dee's conception is shown below:

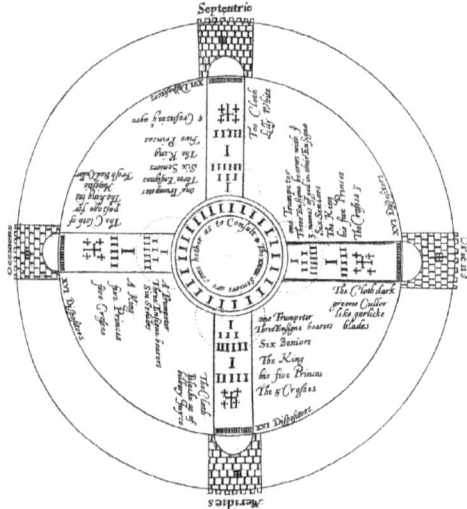

I am very critical of those who use the watchtowers in Wicca, especially those who ask guardians or angels to guard their rites because they, like the LBRP, use a strict Abrahamic view of the world and I honestly believe that this has no place in Wicca. Grimassi and several others claim that these watchers are ancient Babylonian or Greek, but the winds and their associated gods are NOT "the watchers," and are not conceptualized as watching mankind. They are an Abrahamic invention.

I sincerely believe[17] one of the worst travesties of Ceremonial Magic in Wicca is the addition of the Watchtowers of John Dee (and Enochian Magic) to the erecting the temple rite. The audacity of such an act borders on Diabolism, but generally occurs out of pure ignorance. I think the Diabolism excuse would be better. Dee and his lot flourished as England left Catholicism behind. It is not wholly inaccurate to say that these early Anglicans believed that the Vatican had top secret magical resources, placing the Catholics in the same category that earlier Christians placed the Jews, as a secret society withholding magical powers from the rest of the world.

---

[17] Much of the next few pages have been published elsewhere in my introduction to *The Ritual of the Compass Rose.*

One of the remaining cultural beliefs of this group, other than anti-Catholic prejudice, is that Latin somehow reverberates differently in the mind and therefore empowers magic differently, which is why many modern things employ Latin to sound more magical. "*Expecto Patronum,*" anyone?

Like Vaughan and the elementalists, Dee's magical system is rooted in the idea that humanity was kicked out of paradise for its wickedness and that magic is one way their god, who is supposed to be omnibeneficient, seeks to make things right by his errant creations. Dee and his contemporaries, like earlier mages, thought that there was a massive top secret magic of the Jews that they received directly from their god. Where they differed from earlier mages was they believed that this powerful secret Jewish magic was now[18] known to Christians, only now the people who were in charge of keeping it top secret were Catholics, especially spooky Spanish Catholics. The idea of top secret Catholic magic persists to this day, and it's a good hook to sell books with. The theory can be summed up this way: If an organization exists that any individual is not a member of (Masons, Pagans, Catholic Clergy, Jews, etc.) then the assumption is that the organization has top secret powers that warrant the exclusion of others. It's silly, really.

So Dee, fancying himself a scientist, "discovered" that by performing the right mathematical equations and revealing the complicated shapes of his own versions of the Solomanic "pentacles," he could cause the archangels to speak with the body of a channel, in his case Edward Kelley[19].

These "angels" spoke in a language which he called Enochian, and included a related symbology. The most important revelations of these angels are called The Enochian Calls. It is without a doubt that at least some of the things the angels requested of Dee through Kelley were of Kelley's own making, including a wife-swapping episode, but believing the angels were real is a vital part of Enochiana, so I'll let that lie there where it may.

---

[18] In the 14th and 15th centuries, that is.
[19] In some of his less lucid moments, Crowley claimed to be the reincarnation of Edward Kelley.

If you were not raised Christian, or you were raised in a tradition of Christianity that believed in a *Sola Scriptura* version of the mythos, you may have missed the Christian mythology that John Dee worked within, although it was common knowledge in his time, and fed numerous plays and poems, some of which, such as Dante's Inferno and Marlowe's Faustus, are still pretty good reading. Here, then, is a brief introduction to how the Christian world of John Dee worked:

In the beginning, there was a great big void. God was alone and decided that there should be more in the world, so he spoke all things into existence with the power of his words. He placed all things into a system where the sun and the moon and stars worked in a logical order. He was, in short, the architect of his universe.

Eventually, God decided the universe needed population. He created the angels, and set them to keeping the world running. The angels did not have free will, so they obeyed him without thinking about it. The lack of ability to make decisions made these angels boring, so to serve as intermediaries between him and the angels, he created the archangels, who were stronger and smarter than the angels, and had free will.

There are hundreds of these archangels, but there are eight that are important to the Christian tradition, and those are Michael, Gabriel, Anael, Oriphiel, Raphael, Samael, Zachariel and, you guessed it, Lucifer.

Now, you have to bear in mind that Christian mystics literally spent days arguing over the nature of these angels. That's where we get the whole "angels on the head of a pin," metaphor. Some taught that Michael was not an angel at all, but an incarnation of God, a sort of mortal form he wore when he went to speak to mankind or do other tasks. In some of these traditions, Michael was actually the first thing God created, a sort of prototype of both mankind and Jesus. In the "let us make them in our image" debate, it is argued God is talking about himself and at least Michael when he uses the collective plural…but, anyways…

God created the world in layers. At the uppermost layer he abides in a physical form, and he collects all good things to him. In the lowest layer, the world farthest from him, lurks the stuff he dislikes and pushes away. He assigns his creation into these layers based on how well they turned out. One day, one of the archangels, Lucifer, gets sick of being a slave and takes over the lowest levels, deciding it's better to be a king of a terrible place than a slave in paradise. This only strengthens the gradient of the layers of the universe, making evil reside at the lowest levels, farthest from God, and God residing at the highest.

Eden is created fairly high up in the layered universe, and it is given its own equivalent of angels and archangels. Elementals are created to do the smallest tasks, and small animals, insects and the like are created to do their tasks as well. Unlike the elementals, angels and archangels, animals and insects are given the capacity to breed as they so wish. They are sent to fill the layers of the universe, with the ones with God's approval in the highest layers and the ones God hates the most at the lowest levels.

Mankind is created to fill Eden with life, and given the job to keep Eden under control and give order to the place. The first human gets a variety of mates before a female human is developed. He lives, happily, in his garden for hundreds of years, naming things, talking with the trees and animals (because everything in Eden is sentient) and living happily without clothes or shame in a world where food just grows on the branches and the water flows clear from the rock.

One day, one of the other sentient creatures in the garden, a dragon[20], one of the most beautiful of the creations, convinces the humans to eat the fruit of the only tree in the whole of the garden God said not to eat. This pisses God off, and the dragon and his descendants end up with no wings or feet or voices, doomed to crawl about on their belly (now they are snakes). They are banished to the lowest levels of the universe, and made servants of Lucifer.

Humans are also punished, although less so. Women are given periods and painful childbirth and the protohumans are thrown down out of Eden and land in the central area of the layers of the universe, where they are still commanded to be fruitful and multiply, but now they are encountering the other humans cast out of Eden, animals that are dumb and violent and other things. Now, instead of keeping an ordered place in order, they must bring order to chaos.

Humans are still important, though. By making their new layer of the universe a reflection of heaven, they prevent the lower layers from growing. Unfortunately, since the laws of the universe are the same in all layers (as above, so below) it is always easier to descend

---

[20] It is often said this is Satan, but in traditional Christian mythology these are two different instances of bad guys.

into hell than it is to ascend into heaven, so mankind keeps giving in to temptation and failing.

First, God tries to help by giving people special powers, including talking with the animals and talking with the elementals and angels.[21] When that fails, he leaves signs in the world about the order of things[22] that skilled man can interpret. Still, mankind is evil, and is starting to not believe in God, so God takes a few of the descendants of the refugees from Eden, and many of the good animals, and puts them on a boat, and drowns most of the rest of the world[23]. This gives his new people a chance to make a paradise out of the world, but soon they are returning to their old tricks.

When he destroyed the world, he promised he would not do it again, so now God limits himself to only destroying places where the evil is REALLY bad, and very concentrated. At first, he just uses his usual powers, earthquakes, lightning, raining brimstone, but this makes him really annoyed, and he gets sick of being the executioner, so he puts archangels and sky-riding powers called ἵππος, horses, to work.

The descendants of the original Eden refugees and the survivors of the Flood have a host of abilities at their hands to avoid being there when the powers ride through. They can talk to God, they have rituals and words that get his attention, and over time they've learned some of the words he used to speak the Universe into existence and a few other techniques to be safe, and they have a few near misses. God gives gifts to some of the people, like prophetic dreams, to help them out over time[24].

Since he doesn't want to spend his time looking at bad guys, he takes four of his best archangels and places them in towers at the four edges of the central layer of the universe. From these towers, they keep an eye out for sin so he can surround himself only with the good things. He places the worst of all things, including his four horsemen, in the towers. Even the dragon that started the whole thing in Eden is chopped into four parts and one piece is placed in each tower. People are warned that they are being watched, but they still continue to stray.

In a last-ditch effort to save some of mankind from the impending opening of the towers, which will release the four horse-

---

[21] As per Thomas Vaughan, *Clavicula Salomonis*, etc.
[22] Mostly Jakob Böhme, here.
[23] Mostly Genesis
[24] Vaughan, Exodus, Genesis, Revelation.

men and give the world over to evil, God inseminates a human female of the descendants of the Eden refugees and goes around in a human form telling them where they've strayed. He's especially concerned about the leaders of the remaining Edenites and their straying from the law[25].

Much blood has been spilled, and the old magic that God works with says that blood needs blood. To clean the slate, he sacrifices himself and this allows him to better understand the universe as mankind does. He is shown temptation, and he takes pity on mankind, giving them the chance to come and reside with him after their stint on earth is through, even if they were not perfect. The Guardians of the Watchtowers are quelled, and they are told to keep looking, but to keep the reins tight on the horsemen and the other criminals and bad things that live in the towers. His stint as a human has packed these towers with the wicked who are too wicked to trust to hell, because they might escape…

A couple of Herods, an Apostle[26] and half of the elders of the province of Judea are added to the towers in this time period. The creation of such good in the universe as his own son/avatar meant that evil had to be added to the universe in the same amount, or the material plane of earth would be demolished by shifting in its place in the layers. God must fight a constant battle to keep things where they belong, because that's how the system he made operates, and he likes it that way, but it still has rules.

This new evil demigod, an anti-Christ, is kept in the towers. The archangels, though, are creatures of total free will, and while God is forgiving, they are not, and if the world gets evil enough, they will open the gates and let out the four horsemen, the antichrist, the powers of fire, water, earth and air and a host of baddies that live in the towers. Before that happens, God will give a bunch of signs to his chosen people, who may be spared.

Once the evil has had its way with the material plane, it will turn on itself and a new era of goodness and a new Eden will be created. All good things will be housed in the new Eden and the cycle will start again.

---

[25] Mostly the gospels and Revelation, here.
[26] Or not. There is a fairly strong tradition that says that Judas paid blood-for-blood and granted heaven by virtue of the "old laws," that would no longer be in effect shortly after. Whether or not he was there to greet Jesus with Disco angels is not something I wish to discuss in this context.

There are a number of things you must get from this story to understand the mechanism of the magic circle of Dee. First, you must understand that calling the elementals is nonsense even to ceremonial mages. Command of the elementals shows that you have power over an element, and does not have anything to do with the circle but is proof of one's connection to the creator of Eden. It is evidence of one's godliness. Remember, also, that the authors of Christian elemental magic believed that these elementals were absolutely detectable if you could see heat or cold or travel deep in the earth. These were things they expected scientific proof of.

Calling the Guardians of the Watchtowers or the archangels in the magic circle was designed to lend power to your rite by virtue of the eyes of the Guardians. A shade or dead spirit would be compelled to be absolutely truthful because an untruth before the Guardians could result in a one-way trip into the prisons of the towers. You got the guardian's attention by use of their names, which were full of power because they were the names God used to speak them into existence. The Hebrew (and later the Latin) names of these beings and things associated with God were considered to have innate power. Consider the invocation of the Lesser Banishing Ritual of the Pentagram as another example.

The ceremonial magic circle which is often cropped for use in Wicca is a Christian-based creation which uses the powers of the Christian god and the Will of the Wiccan to hold the power and direct it as needed. The proper erecting the temple rite prepares the way to enter into communion with the gods. This Wiccan Temple and the Ceremonial Circle are not compatible, at least not in my view.

That does not stop one from being able to erect the temple with a four-point physical space. Gardner's 1949 circle in the public Book of Shadows does not have a formal invocation of the guardians, but instead mentions exorcising (he's actually *exhorting*, calling upon , not *exorcising*, banishing[27]) creatures of fire and water much more

---

[27] There are little errors like this all through his rites, which many of us find endearing. When confronted with alleged traditionals who have the audacity to pick apart my rites, I take comfort in the little old guy who didn't know the difference between exhort and exorcise whom many of them consider the "master." I'm sure he'd laugh at them, too.

like the traditional indigenous European heraldic spirits than Paracelsus' elementals. This is the Fire and Water of Excalibur, but rather than claim an Arthurian tradition of magic, I sincerely believe that Arthur penetrates British magic because he is the British mythic (epic) hero, and Wicca is in many ways about the mythic journey.

Gardner's circle does not mention air or earth, but does mention "Mighty Ones of the East, South, West, and North," which later authors took to mean the archangels. It is possible to cast a four-point circle that invokes the four points as the four major winds, the four Classical deities of the winds, Fire and Water, Heaven and Hell as in traditional British mysticism or even in terms of personal space, where east is above and west is below. Consider this ritual fragment[28]:

"Fire to my Left, Water to my Right, Heaven above, Hell to fight."

While the text might not work with many temples, because of the imagery, if you alter the text to work with the Wiccan "circle" rite, it might read:

"Fire to my Left, Water to my Right, Air above, Earth below."

Now, this doesn't rhyme, and it does put air in the north[29], but if you understand the idea of the left and the right in magic, and the idea in magic of fire as destructive and water as creative, you see these four points as referring not merely to directions but also to the powers each person holds within–the powers of creation and destruction and the powers of the gods–birth and death. In the Triarchy of Man, this is especially well designed, as the powers of creation and destruction (in the physical sense of building and tearing down, not the life sense) are powers humankind shares with animals, and the powers of birth and death (in the literal sense, the power to make other things replicate) are the powers we share with the gods. This arrangement of the classical elements, from air to fire, earth to water, not only is stronger in the ceremonial magic sense, but is based on logic, not on the location of some Christian angels.

---

[28] Non-Wiccan and name withheld by request, the heaven and hell here are used in the classical understanding as "heavens" meaning the place where the gods reside and also the sky and hell meaning the underworld, where ALL go when they die, not the Christian "heaven and hell."

[29] Which has support, for other reasons:
http://www.geocities.com/Athens/Forum/7280/rethink.html

Earth opposes Air, Fire opposes Water, and a circle based on this opposition is more stable to me than the traditional one, even the one used by UEW and appearing in All One Wicca.

Physical temples don't need to be based on four, however. A physical temple can be very firmly created by marking three points, five (as in the pentagram,) six, eight (as in the octogram I used in *Compass Rose*) or even in a continuous line along the circle itself. The differences tend to be cosmetic unless you are working with energy, and those who've read *Rose* know I prefer an octogram and invoking my nefarious privateer ancestors when working with energy.

With the physical temple, the most important thing, other than the ability to draw a straight or curved line, is that you understand any mythology you are building into it. You must know your myths like a brick layer knows his bricks and mortar, for they are the foundation of your physical temple.

Practice:

Using an octogram as a physical temple with three paths (from *Compass Rose*.)

This ritual fragment shows a way of establishing a physical space without using elements at all. You learned how to declare your intent in the previous chapter, and you can use that here.

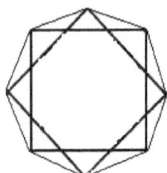

If outside, use stakes and ropes to mark out the eight points and their lines, or pour a rough estimate of the shapes out with something harmless, like flour or sawdust. Clearly mark the points of the winds. If indoors, use tape. It is permissible in this case to make your outer circle into an octagon, left.

Place a glass containing water at each point and float a floating candle within it. By doing this, you cancel out the effect of the fire at each point, rendering the elements at each point inherently stable. Remember that the compass rose does not associate the elements with directions, as the traditional circle does, but instead invokes all elements as being of one place.

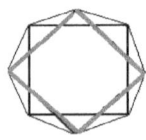

Visualize a line of blackness as you walk clockwise from the north along the diamond path. See it shielding the space within. I have highlighted the diamond path in gray to the left. The diamond path represents those actions that are selfless, doing primarily for others, but do not confuse it with actions that are purely good. When you have finished, stand facing each of the compass points and intone the first syllable of each of the four cardinal winds.

Step to the northwest, and walk the square path (the other square in the octogram) counterclockwise. This should be visualized as blue. The square path represents those actions that are selfish, doing primarily for yourself. Do not confuse this with evil, however. When you have finished, stand facing each of the cross compass points and intone the first syllable of the remaining winds.

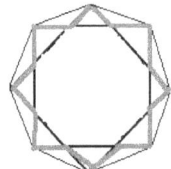

Step to the north and walk the outer path, left, visualizing red light. This is the path of the outside, of relationships with other people and physical entities. The outer path is the path of strength that comes from outside one's self and should not be seen as anything else. When you reach the center, announce who you are and what you are doing there. The blessing of the space should follow shortly. Feel free to announce this to your participants at this time.

Next, walk the inner path, the octagon at the heart of the octogram, visualizing white light. This is the path of the self, and represents the relationships to your gods and your ancestors. When finished, stand at the center and say an appropriate prayer or intonation, obviously, you have to find this within.

Chapter Four: Temples of the Mind

Earlier, I discussed that the well-trained will can create a version of reality so compelling that nature, abhorring dissonance, will attempt to bring the world into harmony with it. While this is hard to do on the big scale, it's something we already know our minds can do with our mental and emotional states. If the spiritual dimension of the temple rite is rightness with the gods and the physical dimension rightness in space and time, then the mental dimension is rightness with oneself, and it is centered within the mind.

In UEW, the first major version of the elemental tetragram circle that most students learn involves guided meditations upon the elemental states. These visualizations are important because they are a quick and easy route to the energetic dimension of the erecting the temple rite for most people and can usually clue a student in to that aspect of the rite even if they never manage to meet another Wiccan. In many ways, the mental is the doorway to the energetic, because every action one does is mental first, converted from thought to deed in the brain. Understanding the mental leads to understanding all of the ways in which we erect the temple, including the energetic.

Visualization is one mental aspect of erecting the temple that is generally easy to teach, fast to learn and easy to place in a self-directed format. It's far from the only way of using the mind to build the temple and similarly not the only way of building a mental temple. It is one way to prepare the way, however.

We mentally prepare the way by taking the spiritual and physical preparations discussed earlier and placing them into the mind. Our minds, like our temples, must be open to the gods and ancestors and worthy of their presence while simultaneously separating the mind into "worship time" and "not-worship time." It's easy to see how this parallels the creation of physical and spiritual temple spaces, since your ideal mindset should be a reflection of the world outside of it and vice versa.

While most of the problems discussed with the spiritual dimension are paralleled in the mental—preparing the way *inside* in a manner that the gods, your ancestors and your physical self can live with—there is no parallel for the gathering of will, mental selves and concentration that the mental aspect involves.

If you are fortunate enough to have a transparent inner process, collecting your mental toolkit and building the temple within is not that difficult. Most people, however, do not have a particularly transparent inner process, and don't have access to how their mind goes from one thought to the other, making teaching the mental construction of the temple difficult.

The easiest way to begin to make your inner mental process transparent is to identify and learn to understand the schema your mind uses to sort the world. Many of us use a verbal schema, a sort of inner dialog or inner text where the brain is carrying on rather coherently and if you focus on just that inner dialog you'll find it's something you can document, using a journal or blog to write about your thoughts. People with this type of verbal processing tend to be readers and writers and best come to an understanding of their processes via writing about their reactions to things, descriptions of things and emotions.

Most people use multiple schemae to come to an understanding of the world. If you tend to process the world via emotions, for example, you may still use words to describe the emotions. If you find your journal entries are mostly emotion words, you should probably focus on finding words that accurately describe your emotions, turning a process that may be very difficult to express into something more coherent and thus more transparent.

Many people don't use words at all in their inner processes, but images and memory fragments. The equivalent of journaling for these people is often making collages or scrapbooking. Sometimes sketches help as well, but the process of making *new* images really doesn't tap the same places as the process of organizing images into a coherent system. The goal in any exercise in making your internal process transparent should be in understanding how your brain moves from one image or thought to another.

Coming to understand the process is vital to erecting the mental temple because humans, like termites, are naturally builders. Young children put things in lines and towers, circles and curves. Adults do this as a way of organizing our world; it soothes us, making us feel more in control of an often loud and chaotic universe. We make lists, chant, drum, sing, write, clean and meditate to build little spheres of control around ourselves where the universe acts with reasonable laws and understandable ramifications. This is natural, instinctual, and something we should use when creating the temple.

Visualization is generally an easy road to using these instincts to create the temple because it is a pure brain exercise. You block out sensory data and use your mind to touch, taste, feel, remember, imagine, hear and, above all else, *see* the temple around you and before you, and your will and the universe help make it one.

Let's imagine you know your inner process and because of that you know that *you* tend to separate your mind into work-mind and play-mind. With that in mind, you'd want the temple to be a place that is a union of both, literally using your whole mind. To accomplish this, you might first do a visualization or other exercise that involves the play-mind and then another which involves the work-mind, and then a third that involves both. You'd have to customize the technique to your understanding of your inner process, obviously, because the only one who knows your mind is *you*.

When a group or tradition wants to teach the mental aspect of erecting the temple, they tend to create generic inner processes that work for multiple people and encourage the individual student to explore both the generic inner processes and their inner process. These processes tend to parallel an aspect of the temple rite, such as invoking internal elements or internally reenacting a mystery rite. It is important that the external temple rite matches the internal rite, however, so if you aren't casting a tetragram circle using the classical elements don't use them in your inner rite. Likewise, if the journey mystery rite isn't a part of your theology, don't add it here.

The simplest mental temple rite can be often be accomplished by walking around the circle visualizing light building beside you. Try to imagine the light floating behind you in a long trail, settling beside your footsteps. With each successive path, the light should rest atop the previous path, and you can drag your hand along the circle as you walk, touching it and manipulating it. Once you've built this to your specifications, you can stand at the center of it and practice manipulating it— raising and lowering it, changing the color, moving it. In minimalist temples, discussed later, you may erect this imagined temple from the center, merely calling it into being with a thought and perhaps a hand movement.

Once you have this mental circle created, imagine things that are pressing at this point in time floating in the light. Those things that are appropriate to the time and space of the rite should stick to the interior surface of your light. Those things that are inappropriate for the time and space of the rite should be sucked through the light and into the time and space outside of it. If you are primarily a verbal thinker, try removing things from the space by telling them "be gone."

> To me I call righteousness, justice, strength, trust and love. Be gone jealousy, be gone anger, be gone wasters of time and energy. Now is the time for the gods, here is the place for our rite.
>
> From me fly, all things without mercy, capricious beasts of rage or loss. To me harken all things of grace. Now is the time, here is the place.[30]

The ritual fragment above is spoken as part of an erecting the temple rite to bring the mental temple from the mental into the physical. Words have power, and when directed with will they have even more power. By reciting these words inside the mind you help organize the thoughts into an appropriate ritual mindset, by speaking them you invest them with power, because they now are physical sensations and audible sounds.

Ideally the mental temple is something you practice until you have it so established that you can summon it up without much

---

[30] Circle casting rite, source withheld, used with permission.

work. It generally helps to be able to create a path inside your mind, a series of steps that you take in an attempt to have an inner journey to the temple. The aforementioned elemental visualizations are one such step. The student practices, in turn, being one with air, fire, earth and water so that in the tetragram circle as each element is call the student goes through the mental process of the elemental states.

This process, which is detailed in *All One Wicca*, is especially helpful for those who are trying to make the step from Solitary practice to the casting of the energetic dimension of the circle, as the skills each visualization teaches go into that process. As stated earlier, the circle does not necessarily have to follow those four classical elements, and it is for this reason that my mental practice circle uses the visualization of a tree. I want to both instruct you in the techniques of preparing the way inside the mind and try to show you how to think "outside the circle" in terms of the construction of the temple.

Ideally, erecting the mental temple involves as much of the mind as possible, and therefore as much of the brain as possible. There should be a memory or recall aspect, a physical aspect, an emotional aspect and several sensory aspects. One particularly effective way of doing this is by doing a mental walkthrough of the erecting the temple rite. Remember, always, that you are creating a compelling reality within your mind, a reality so compelling that nature is moved to comply with it.

Practice:

This version uses speech and visualization. You may find yourself learning it best by recording it and playing it back. Dried leaves will work, but green ones are best. If leaves are not available, adapt the rite using appropriate imagery.

> *Stand in a place that you have cleared and cleaned. Create a physical circle out of leaves that you have harvested on your own. You should have another small pile of leaves with you...pick them up. Close your eyes.*
>
> *Slowly drop the leaves to the floor. Focus on the sound that they make as they fall and land. Hear the sound of the leaves and*

remember a time when you were in a forest, even if it was just to get the leaves for this practice. Try to remember intensely the sound of leaves upon leaves. Listen to the rustle as they pile upon each other. Practice this until you hear only the leaves when you do it. Focus upon the leaves as intently as you will focus upon the voice of the divine.

Kneel on the floor and smell the leaves. Focus on the hints of different flavors the leaves present. Smoky, dark and earthy or green and fresh, remember a time when you smelled leaves in the forest. Try to hear the leaves in the forest as you smell them. What do they smell like? What do they sound like?

Spread out your hands and touch the leaves. Feel the veins in them, the stems, and the delicate edges. Run your fingers over a leaf until you can picture it in your mind. Open your eyes look at the leaf, note the colors, the textures, the shape.

Think of what you know about how a tree forms. It may start as a seed, nut, acorn or cutting, but it always starts small and moves to big. Think of a time when you were small. Remember what it was like to have to stretch to get something off of a table top or shelf. Stand, slowly, and stretch your arms up. You are a growing human, and a growing tree. Stretch your arms up above your head and then slowly lower them so they are your branches.

Visualize a glow that starts in the center of your body and slowly moves out to your extremities. It goes down through your feet to pool at the edges of the circle, and drips like rain from your fingers. The circle is your drip line, and everything underneath pulses with your energy. Rotate slowly, feeling the boundary at the edge of your fingers.

Turn your face towards the sky and imagine a fall of brightly lit spring rain descending upon you. Try to feel it on every inch of your skin, running down, making your circle stronger and stronger. Bring your arms in, hugging yourself. Feel the energy build until it sparkles like static in the air around you.

Thrust your arms out and exhale sharply, forcing the energy to escape the boundaries of your circle. You are a star, igniting for the first time, bursting into life!

This visualization is designed to help you come to understand how the energy of your mind works. In the contemporary erecting the temple rite, you may choose to use it for raising power or merely as practice in the way the mind influences the rite itself. Don't worry if you don't feel the rain or see the leaves, what is particularly important is that you understand the inner journey and the transitions the mind makes. It is this transition, from outside life to life within the temple that is important.

Chapter Five: Temples of Tradition

Have you ever typed a word that ended in "io" and automatically added an n to it? Have you ever moved a dresser or a table and found yourself walking into it in broad daylight? Have you ever walked into a freshly painted room you've never seen before and known exactly where furniture belongs? Have you ever walked in the forest randomly and discovered you were on a path you had no way of knowing the existence of?

In each of these instances you experienced a case of the rehearsal effect. In the first two instances your mental map of the English language and your mental map of your house differed from reality. In the latter two, you followed subconscious cues about direction and space, mental maps based not on your experience but the experiences of others, including the designers and former tenants of the room and the forest and those who walked the paths before you.

Just as people walking over the same path in a forest repeatedly will eventually change the forest around it, so too do rehearsed and repeated actions create paths in reality. The wise Wiccan takes advantage of this when preparing the way for communion with the divine because just as we might build a road to facilitate the journey of people from one place to another, we can build a road in reality that allows the gods to interact with us better by using the same actions repeatedly and the actions that others, through the paths of human time, have used.

One mechanism to do this is to use reconstructed ancient rites and mysteries. This can create an ethical dilemma, however, because many reconstructed rites require a context that a Wiccan may or may not share. In addition, the validity of a reconstructed rite may depend wholeheartedly on who is doing the reconstruction. Using a fully reconstructed rite, then, requires a lot of research and practice with the understanding that it might prove useless. You may discover in the end that the entire rite you've studied is impossible to use in a respectful way and discard it altogether.

A way to avoid this is to use ritual fragments that essentially lack context or have a particularly Wiccan context. While I have spoken a lot at this point about moving away from traditional rites, this is one reason to not do so, and perhaps the best understanding of this dichotomy is to understand that I do not, personally, oppose the use of traditional rites, but instead I oppose the use of such rites in a way that lacks context, or the use of rites that are composed in a way that is disrespectful of the ritual language's context.

The reason tradition is the last of the four dimensions I am featuring is because it is possible to prepare the way in a manner that is traditionally valid but fails on all other levels. Therefore an understanding of the other levels before the traditional is discussed is required.

If you are interested in using the personal level of tradition to strengthen your rite, you can use the rehearsal effect, using the same steps[31], physical movements and the like to strengthen the path through reality between laying the foundation of the temple rite and completing it. You can also use cue worlds and ritual phrases. These phrases, like the typing example given earlier, should bring to mind immediate responses.

The simplest cue phrase in Wicca is "Blessed Be[32]," which comes from a ritual fragment known as the fivefold kiss. Blessed Be is problematic because repeated use of a cue phrase or word out of context can significantly weaken the bonds of the phrase to the inner and outer world. If you use Blessed Be as a greeting, and do not imply all of the Fivefold Kiss when you say it, you are reducing the power of it at a traditional level. Whether this weakens it through all of time or just as an individual practice is a matter of speculation that I don't wish to comment upon at this time, but I don't personally see Blessed Be as an acceptable code for "Look at me I'm Wiccan."

Formal English, Latin and Greek all have possibilities as cue words. They are useful because you're not going to use them in common speaking. I don't know about you, but I don't go around

---

[31] In Ceremonial Magic, and to a lesser degree, Wicca it is customary to vary the circle or temple rite to anchor it to this space and time. An example might be "I have come here on the night of the full moon in the height of summer to…"

[32] Those who have never encountered Wiccans offline sometimes pronounce this Blest Be, but it should be pronounced to rhyme with "Jess, Ed, Me."

saying "Thee" and "Thy" even though I know the proper way to place them into the English language. In ritual, however, the use of the archaic, when done in a sensical, rational manner, can add a whole new dimension of reality to a rite.

Although they can often be easily researched, I think most of us *know* when we've stumbled upon a word or phrase that has been used in a special manner repeatedly in the past. It has a distinct feeling in the mouth, almost as if the word is more than a sound, something edible, tangible, that you can taste, feel and touch in addition to hearing and saying. They can be discovered and achieved with practice as a solitary, more than any other aspect of the traditional circle, although it requires a little discernment at the start.

The use of rhyme and meter in the circle is largely an outgrowth of this knowledge. Many of those who have seriously studied Shakespeare, especially as actors, have found the rhythm of Shakespearian plays following them off of the stage, as the hidden drumbeat of iambic pentameter remained pounding in their head long after the curtain fell. There is no doubt in the minds of those who have experienced this that iambic pentameter is something special in the English language, one of a few meters seemingly designed to empower the words and resonate them in a way that strengthens their intent and the will behind them.

There is no doubt that the use of rhyme and meter can be beneficial to the rite, although the over use of it and AAAA and ABAB rhyme patterns tend to remind people more of Dr. Seuss than liturgy, and should probably be reconsidered.

The use of traditional liturgy and fragments used by Wiccans for over sixty years can help strengthen a temple's anchor to reality and make it right with one's ancestors as well as with the gods, but it must be done in a way that does not create discord in the temple. For example, a circle rite from the 1970s using the Christian Watchtowers, while benefiting from the vibrational energy of existence in time, still suffers from enough discord to reduce the reality of the rite, especially if the one doing the rite has mixed feelings or negative feelings about Christianity.

One of the Wiccan's hardest tasks is finding a balance between traditional practice and current need and a middle ground between disposing of old rites that disrupt the spirit of the temple with their naïve collection of unrelated sources and creating rites that don't resonate through Wiccan history at all. I understand how this creates the compulsion to search outside of Wicca for stuff to add to the temple rite, but I genuinely believe that the context of a source is as important as the source itself. If the source's context would not be right with the gods, then the source's material is not right with the gods.

Practice:

Rather than provide a definitive exercise and technique for this section, I have an exercise that I have given in the past to students, that they have found particularly edifying. There is no one right way to complete the exercise, but you should have enough discernment to know if you've done it wrong.

The Solitary Five-Fold Kiss:

Given the typical (female) five fold kiss (below) construct a solitary ritual fragment that accomplishes the same purposes as the kiss itself at an individual level. Obviously, the welcoming of another into the circle part of the kiss is not appropriate, so begin by figuring out what purposes the kiss fulfills for each participant in the ritual, which purposes are appropriate for the solitary ritual, and which are not. Once you've crafted your technique, apply it to a ritual and record the results.

"Blessed be thy feet, that have brought thee in these ways.
Blessed be thy knees, that shall kneel at the sacred altar.
Blessed be thy womb, without which we would not be.
Blessed be thy breasts, formed in beauty.
Blessed be thy lips, that shall utter the Sacred Names."

Chapter Six: Holistic Temples

The term holistic is defined in part by Merriam-Webster as "relating to or concerned with wholes or with complete systems rather than with the analysis of, treatment of, or dissection into parts[33]." Holistic temples are exactly that, temple rites that incorporate the energetic, the spiritual, the physical, the mental and the traditional as a whole, rather than as five individual pieces. While the five pieces help to understand the whole, the rite itself is more than the sum of its parts.

To understand the construction of the holistic temple rite one must first understand the parts and then understand how they work together in a complex lattice to build something exquisite. For an example, let us prepare a three-point coven temple rite using the land, sea and sky and Roman deities. Obviously this rite is going to be easy to adapt to Celtic or Greek pantheons, since the number three is more readily placed in these pantheons than the number four. I've prepared this rite as a sort-of walkthrough, with the idea that you'd read the entire rite, rather than try to do it yourself, so forgive my liberties as I lapse into second person prose.

It is a fall night in the Great Lakes region of the United States, Halloween to the non-Pagans. The air feels cool but not cold on your skin as you and five of your closest friends gather on a hill top. At the center of the top of the hill is a campfire, ringed by fat tumbled lake stones. Hardwood logs crackle and burn as the sun descends, the smoke rising straight up in the windless evening.

At the moment the sun vanishes and the upper reaches of sky descends into indigo, the priestess of the group, a leader but nonetheless an equal, calls out in a crisp voice that rings across the hillside in the cooling air. "It is the turning of the year," she says, "fall is half spent and winter approaches on this, the Eve of November. Hear our rites, all ye good gods, and attend us this night if it be your will. We have come to watch the wheel turn once more."

This part of the rite announces the beginning of the temple. By bringing up the time of the ritual and its purpose, the ritual is an-

---

[33] http://m-w.com/dictionary/holistic

chored in space and time. I have chosen November Eve because it is the closest Wicca comes to the "Christmas Catholics," in that few Wiccans will not have attended at least one such rite. The priestess has separated the ritual from the time before the ritual both with her words and by waiting until the moment the sun has disappeared before beginning. The effect of this is mental, affecting the participants, as well as spiritual, affecting the ancestors and the gods. Her use of ritual inflection[34], as well as any hand gestures, fulfills the physical aspect. The use of specific ritual language (Eve of November, Watch the Wheel turn) resonates on the traditional level, while the invocation of the gods to attend if it be their will is both traditional and a way of preparing the way in accordance with the gods.

The priestess places a large bundle of herbs upon the fire, and a puff of smoke rises up. "Jupiter, lord of the heavens, if it be thy will, look down upon us and grant us your attention for this brief rite." *The priestess takes a firebrand from the fire, ends smoking, and walks around the hilltop in a circle, around you and the other participants. The branch pops and crackles as a shower of sparks surrounds you.* "Let this path be a barrier to all that would not come to you with faces unmasked and hearts opened." *You and all the other participants sing:* "We pray this night to do what's right, let those who'd wrong us all take flight."

The priestess finishes her circumnavigation and returns to her earlier spot. She holds up a large goblet of sea water. "Neptune, lord of the seas that surround us and provide for us, if it be thy will, look to us and grant us your attention for this brief rite." *She sprinkles the water around the circle as she had with the sparks from the firebrand.* "Let this path be a barrier to all that would not come to you with pure thoughts and honest intention." *You and the other participants sing:* "We gather upon this hill to do thy will, let none remain who'd mean us ill."

The priestess returns to the spot again and holds up an iron staff. "Lord of Wealth, unseen Pluto, protector of the dead, if it be thy will, look up upon us and grant us your attention for this brief rite."

---

[34] Those who have not studied theatre often find ritual inflection difficult, but it is, essentially, speaking clearly in a manner that is loud but not sharp. Done well, the pitch and timbre vibrates with the surrounding area, adding to the force of the rite.

She drags the staff along the ground, turning over a furrow of earth. "Let this line mark the boundary between we, your servants and those who would not come forward in perfect love and perfect trust." You and the others sing, "Like the phoenix arising from ashes and dust, we come with perfect love and trust."

The calling of the three domains is repeated with the wives of the gods, Juno, Salacia and Proserpina. This is followed by an invocation to "*All the great gods who were known to our ancestors,*" who are asked to "*bless this rite if you will,*" and are sheepishly told. "*If we give offense, be assured it is accidental, for we worship in a time where the streams of your ways are muddied. We try to do what is right, but we are mere humans, and therefore imperfect.*"

This fulfills the purpose of welcoming the gods as best you can, while not putting yourself on an equal footing with them. One must wonder at those Wiccans who order the gods to attend them like puppies, or who demand that the gods watch them, like a three year old going "Mommy, look!" over and over again. That obviously does not encourage the gods to view you favorably.

The three-prong use of Land, Water and Sky in this ritual is used to mark the boundaries of the world, and the boundaries of the circle. By marking the world as divided into these three realms, the people erecting the temple are saying "The world is composed of these three things, and this temple is of all three."

At the same time, this temple prepares the people within it mentally. They have agreed to mean no ill to each other, to do what's right and to attend in Perfect Love and Perfect Trust. This last term is a trifecta—Traditional, Mental and Spiritual. It sings a song in the mind, a song that the experienced Wiccan should know.

In the case of this particular rite, the calling of the gods and the three realms is followed by declarations of each participant as to their purpose. One might say, for example, "*I am Jack, son of Paul and Jane, one of the Wica. I have come here this night to watch the wheel turn and to honor the passing of my grandfather, Nate. May his light shine in the afterlife as it shone in this life.*"

The announcement of who you are and what your purpose is strengthens the mental bond, but it also prepares the way physically. You are not passively entering the temple of another's hand, but building it with your own will as well. Ideally, you're telling both others and yourself why you are there, building levels of reality upon the temple within you and making the temple outside of yourself a true reflection of it.

You begin a slow chant, not really words, but sounds, it begins low in your throat as you and the others walk slowly around the circle, arms down. After you've rotated three times you stand, facing the center and raise your arms slowly as you raise the volume. The air crackles around you, the hairs on your arms lift, and you each cry out the name of one of the six deities invoked in the temple rite in your loudest voice. The air seems to rush out of the space of the temple.

After a moment, the priestess's voice rings out in the silence. "Now we stand in a temple between the worlds. Of Land but not Land, Of Air but not Air, Of Water, but not Water. Let the turning of the wheel be honored!" The November Eve rite begins.

All of the dimensions of the temple are used in this rite. The Physical, the Mental, the Spiritual, the Energetic and the Traditional. The way is prepared within each participant and outside of them in a manner in accordance with the will of the gods. The November Eve rite then can occur without hesitation.

It should be noted that while this rite easily holds and allows for the release of energy, it's not designed to protect from evil forces or remove the temple from our plane of existence. There are a number of reasons why people claim temple rites do these things, but rather than refute those reasons, I think we should reevaluate what, exactly, the holistic temple does and why it does it.

Energetic Reasons for the Temple Rite:

For many Wiccans, the temple holds energy, which is raised, contained and released in a directed manner. In the example above, the energy was directed to the gods, as a votive sacrifice. In older forms of Wicca, what I consider as pre-ecological Wicca, the energy might be directed towards the turning of the wheel[35]. Regardless of its direction, the energy can be palpably sensed as it is raised and

---

[35] One of the critical distinctions between Early Modern Wicca and Modern Wicca is the change from the belief that humankind is important to help turn the wheel and the belief that the wheel turns whether or not humankind intercedes. While not my particular belief, some also think that energy must *now* be added to turn the wheel in an era of global warming.

directed. The temple, like a bowl, can be refilled and emptied continually until it is taken down at the end of the rite. Contrary to the beliefs of some, I sincerely believe that the "structural" failure of any of the five dimensions is an effective way of taking down the temple, but that will be covered in a later chapter.

The temple, then, does not filter energy, nor prevent the energy from being polluted from energies outside the temple, but instead gathers the energy generated within. This is a more "ecologically friendly" rite, as it does not deplete the inherent energy of a place in any way. It is because of this, however, that the belief that the temple protects from negative energy is inaccurate. The temple is built of the energy that it contains, and fills with the energy brought into it. If you construct it in a place that is negative, then you have brought negativity into it.

This is one reason why a good temple space is cleaned and researched before the temple is even considered. If it is built in a place where it is unwelcome, the energies will be wrong and the foundation of the temple will crumble. This is not to say you can't successfully build a temple where one is not welcome, just that to do so is to limit the success of the temple. Although it may sound snobbish to say so, when I hear of allegedly experienced Pagans casting their circles on sacred native lands against the will of the peoples on that land, I seriously wonder about their inner dialog and their practices. I'm sincere in my belief that most of us would immediately feel if an area was hostile to our temple and deal with that hostility long before we began any working in earnest.

The Physical Reasons for the Temple Rite:

The normal temple rite is going to take place within a space where those within the space are in the rite and those outside the space are not. This is especially important on public land and at gatherings where there are all sorts of energies and events flying around. Just like you might place a blanket to mark out your picnic space, you might use rope, powder or stones to mark out your space.

This creation of boundaries also creates a powerful signal in the brain of the participants. What most people don't know about Ceremonial Magic is that the circle used to contain energies isn't really about a chalk line or powdered oxblood; it's about the mage's will. The line makes a visible signal to the brain, mind and will about where the limits of the energy are. In the case of the temple rite, the physical boundary is a signal to the participants and those that are witnessing it, whoever, or *whatever,* they are. It's a signal that lets all members direct their will and their energy to the same exact point in space, and that's one reason why it's vital in group rites and can be avoided in solitary ones if your concentration is good enough.

The use of physical movement, such as the walk around the circle in the aforementioned hilltop temple, sends a cue to the brain that tells it to wake up and pay attention. One reason I do not recommend the continuous repetition of some hand and body signals that some have placed in their temple rites is that I, personally, have completely zoned out during a ritual that was all about the physical movements. I found myself not thinking about the ritual, but about my next step. That's not a healthy ritual.

Therefore I advocate the use of simple freeform movements, standing, sitting, kneeling, walking, turning, raising and lowering the arms. I also recommend the appropriate use of the "god and goddess" positions, as well as the feet fully planted, arms out "tree" position[36]. These physical movements incorporate the body but aren't about the body. That's not to say that the use of the body in ritual is not a good idea, merely that the body alone is not ideal for building the temple, save for those aspects of the temple that are physical.

The Spiritual Reasons for the Temple:

The temple provides a space to worship, and prepares the way for communion with the divine. In our example rite, the temple rite includes invocation of the gods, but it is also possible to construct the temple *then* invite the gods. In this example, the world is understood as existing on a triarchy- Land, Sea, and Sky. The temple invokes this metaphor by bringing the three things together as one.

Also, the way is prepared by the changes within the participants as they construct the temple and by the way they prepare themselves spiritually. They affirm several times that they came without

---

[36] I wish I could say my family was familiar with this position from my using it often in the circle, but unfortunately they know it most from me dictating where new trees should be planted on our property, where I would spread my branches and go "I'm a tree! I'm happy here!"

the desire to do harm and in an open, appropriate and honest way. Many of the changes contained in the phrase "Perfect Love and Perfect Trust" are spiritual ones, but the changes are implied in the phrase, with the assumption that the Wiccans in the circle know all about the proper level of readiness that the phrase requires.

In group rites, it's not uncommon for the members to perform certain things at the individual level. It's normal to expect that members of a group are completely functional solitaries in their own right, and the preparing of the way they do at the spiritual level should be done both individually and as a group. It is the individual's job to make sure they are right with their ancestors, right with their gods and right with themselves, although the group may have an effect upon it.

The Mental Reasons for the Temple:

Just as the majority of the spiritual aspect of the temple represents a change at the individual level that is acknowledged in the group rite but is nonetheless performed at the individual level, so too the mental aspects are performed inside the individual. The sensory, physical and memory aspects of the mental temple are prepared inside the individual at another time and recalled in the temple rite. These mental aspects tell the mind that it is now in a different world—the ritual world— and that the time to focus with all of one's mental faculties is *now*.

The cues of the temple rite prepare the mental aspect of the individual for worship provided he has prepared himself for the ritual beforehand. Much of the mental aspect discussed in the fourth chapter needs to be accomplished individually before the rite, worked on at the individual level and brought to the front of the mind in the temple itself. Much as a bricklayer brings the skills of bricklaying to the construction of a brick wall, the Wiccan constructing the mental aspect of the temple rite has to bring his skills of mental discipline with him. These skills improve with practice, until they become second nature.

The Traditional Reasons for the Temple:

The traditional aspect of the temple draws upon the power of repetition, the rehearsal effect and the actions of everyone else doing the rite, including those in the past and future, to reverberate through all of reality, time and space and strengthen the ties of the rite and the divine. It prepares the way for the gods in a way that is stronger than just preparing on an individual level, *even* when it is done at the individual level.

The use of traditional words, cues, techniques and skills empower the temple rite and are especially effective if the rite is being performed by a beginner. As you grow in skill, moving away from the traditional tetragram elemental temple rite and into other traditional techniques is to be expected. To vary away from the default you must still know the default, which is why nearly every Wiccan is taught the tetragram elemental temple at the beginning, even if many scholars rightly agree that the elemental correspondences used in Wicca are over-simplistic and naïve.

Chapter Seven: Minimalist Temples

Major life changes are often the catalyst for a change in religion, and it is therefore no surprise that people who are unable to create a large temple rite find themselves converting to Wicca without the benefit of tools, time, large collections of books or mentors. Most of these people are unable to practice large scale because of housing or time restrictions, such as those in most college dorms or military service. Others are paying for actions earlier in their lives with jail time, or even involuntary hospitalization. Regardless of the reason why a minimalist temple is called for, the fact remains that sometimes we can't have knives, candles, incense and other ephemera.

As you may've guessed, I am of the opinion that the mental, energetic and spiritual aspects of the temple rite can be accomplished without a single tool other than a person's will, although I concede that some deities may expect specific cleansing techniques and dress. Minimalist temples, then, focus upon the physical and the traditional without the use of many tools. It is possible to erect these temples without any tools, but unless it is unavoidable it is generally best to learn the use of each tool and remove those you do not need to use in your situation.

The elements, division of the universe into land, sea and air, the Compass Rose and other aspects of the traditional temple rites are as much tools as athamés, incense, goblets or ropes. Just as the skilled practitioner can do without the elemental quarters, despite what others claim, so too can the devoted Wiccan forgo all physical tools, despite what the self-same others claim.

The first set of minimalist temples we'll cover require forethought and planning, and may not be appropriate for those who are limited in their movement in physical space. The first, which we'll call the Sympathetic temple, is probably the easiest, although the materials may be difficult to acquire. While I have used the elemental tetragram for this example, it can also be used in other ways. To better acquaint you with other elemental arrangements, this circle uses air in the *north*, not the east. From north to west on the compass, the elements used herein air, fire, earth, water.

The Sympathetic Temple

Before beginning this rite, find four stones that are long enough to break. If it is vital that you use particular minerals, be certain that the samples you use are capable of being broken or sawed to a point where they can be broken. I recommend thin rods of blue lace agate, red tiger's eye, petrified wood and coral, but that is based upon what I know I can acquire in my area without doing harm to the environment. Any stones will work if their elemental correspondences are strong enough in your mind.

Begin by erecting the temple in your normal way (obviously, you will have to use the elements in this instance if you do not normally. At each erecting of the temple over a long period (I recommend an entire year) let these rods sit at the far points of each quarter. Mark or etch the stones so that the same narrow end of the rod faces the compass point each time. If it's not feasible to do this for a full year, do it at least twice, once during the day and once at night.

For each of the rods, take a few hours to visualize the element the rod represents and run a silk cloth (use a different one for each rod) across the rod. Then travel a significant distance north of where you will be erecting the temple most often and break the northern rod in half. Bury the half of the rod that was at the outer edge of your temple rite so that the tip of the rod faces the direction the rod represents.

As you return to the center, visualize the line of light that connects the piece you keep to the piece you've left behind. Repeat this for each of the other pieces. If it is impossible to travel, you may also try mailing the pieces to people as far on the compass as you can imagine. I don't recommend doing this if the people aren't Wiccan or sympathetic to Wicca.

The pieces of the rod are connected via the magical property of symmetry. You may now take the remaining parts of the rods and lay them out in the compass pattern, broken ends facing outward, and bring forth the temple using nothing more than your mind. It takes work to feel the temple, but using meditation and practice you can feel the compass points and their associated elements.

It is possible to make a small medallion with the milled ends of the rods. Using an appropriate saw and bead drill, remove a small amount of the rod and have the stones threaded on a solar wheel so that the stones turn freely. When the stones are placed, you can invoke the temple by intentionally turning the stones clockwise in each direction and send the temple back by turning them counterclockwise. This medallion may be worn, carried or kept in a safe location, but for all legal purposes it is as much a religious item as a medallion of a saint.

It is also possible to thread these beads on a string, whereupon they are considered the same as a rosary under the law. Obviously, if you use these beads in an inappropriate manner, you've lost all right to possess them.

To erect the temple with the rods, merely use them in all ways as you would use the tools you are doing without. Where you'd light a candle, place the rod momentarily. Where you draw a line, use the tip of the rod. If you are using them to replace such things as an athamé or wand, you may find that using the appropriate elemental correspondences makes the broken rods more effective tools that those they are replacing.

Prayer Bead Temple Rite:

Similar to the rite above, the prayer bead temple rite focuses upon the temple as a form of meditation and prayer. While by no means the only way to use beads, this rite uses the Compass Rose to raise a temple around an individual and prepare the individual to commune with the divine in a small, personal space.

The beads are made of glass, in this case, with silver letter beads from top to bottom labeled T, G, L, S, O, L, P, M. Small beads separate the large ones and prevent them from touching. The beads go [letter]-[clear-1[37]]-[yellow]-[red]-[blue]-[green]-[star[38]]-[black]-[orange]-[gold]-[silver]-[clear-2] and repeat for each letter.

The chant, below, may be performed out loud or within the head, as the situation requires. It is possible to say the temple chant without turning, but a beginner may find it best to say the first part facing north and slowly turn clockwise. The string of beads should be read clockwise to erect the temple and counterclockwise to take it down.

---

[37] The clear stones should be the same, but are marked 1 and 2 to distinguish them.
[38] I use hematite for this.

Letter T: *"Tramontana; winds of change and of beginnings. I am far from home"* (or *'the lands of my ancestors'*) *"and I look to you for beginnings."*

Touch each of the clear-1 stones in succession. One stone per syllable, saying:

Clear-1: *"May I be clear of mind this night/day."*

Touch each of the yellow stones in succession. One stone per syllable, saying:

Yellow: *"In the name of air I call you."*

Repeat for each of the stones as follows:

Red: *"In the name of fire I call you."*

Blue: *"In the water's name[39] I call you."*

Green: *"In the name of earth I call you."*

Star: *"With all of the Wiccans I call you."*

Black: *"With my ancestors I call you."*

Orange: *"With my traditions I call you."*

Gold: *"Before the great gods I call you."*

Silver: *"With the goddesses I call you."*

Clear-2: *"With my will, prepare the way!"*

Pause. Visualize the temple rising around you, becoming more solid with each pass of the beads.

With each of the successive letter stones, summon each of the eight winds,[40] repeat the calling of the nine attributes, above, after each wind. When you reach the end, announce the completion of the temple and proceed with your rite.

Other Minimalist Temples:

It's possible to create any of the traditional "candle lighting" rituals with lights, by drawing chalk symbols on the ground or with visualization. Rites calling for athamés can use fingers instead, and wands, swords and staves can each be replaced by any piece of wood, such as a stick, or even with your hands. It may take work to change a ritual in such a manner, but it is worthwhile every time.

---

[39] Note the rhythm used.

[40] One set of the attributes of the eight winds is given in my *Ritual of the Compass Rose*. This is hardly the only set of attributes, however, and it is vital you associate each wind appropriately for your area as you visualize them. For example, the wind from my *west* brings snow and blows from Canada, which is hardly typical of the United States!

Chapter Eight: Debates in Temple Construction

There are a number of debates in the construction of the temple that I would be severely remiss if I did not discuss. The first and most obvious is the idea that a Wiccan temple rite must be valid for Ceremonial Magic. On this I have but one thing to say: Those of us who know Ceremonial Magic know that it, and Wicca, are not the same thing. Since they are not the same thing, it is nonsense to expect the temple rite to be the same as a Ceremonial Magic circle.

The Size of the Circle:

Gerald Gardner very clearly was basing his nine foot diameter on the (eighteen foot) diameter of the circle in the *Clavicula Salomonis* and his reasons for reducing the diameter by one half are unknown. Many attribute it to simple error, and while I lean that way myself, it's hard to deny that a nine-foot circle fits neatly in most living rooms. It is difficult, however, to place thirteen people around this size circle with a great deal of space, and I recommend that such groups always default to the larger size.

That being said, I sincerely believe that the actual size of the circle should be a matter of convenience, not tradition, even though the nine and eighteen feet circles reverberate through reality strongly because of tradition. I find circles of twelve feet in diameter to be particularly effective at a personal level, based on the size of the spaces I tend to use and the power of the number twelve. In my experience, many groups default to twelve foot diameter circles without even measuring one out, so it's obviously something inside of humanity that makes that distance work.

In short, I would not worry too much about the diameter of any circle used when erecting the temple unless you have a very strong reason for using a particular measurement. I prefer the measure gained by having all participants standing with their fingertips just touching, myself.

The Length of the Temple Rite:

As a general rule, the temple rite should be no more than 30% of the time spent in the ritual. If your temple rites take 40 minutes to set up, and 20 to take down, and your entire ritual is an hour and a half, then you've moved the focus of the ritual from the ritual itself to the temple rite. I try to keep all non-ceremonial magic temple rites under ten minutes in length.

If you feel your temple *must* be very long, then you need to plan an appropriate ritual for such a rite. The temple is preparing the way, not the way itself!

Watchers, Watchtowers, Elementals, Elements:

It should be obvious to you by now that I am firmly against using any of these terms unless you know exactly what they mean and why you are bringing them to the rite. Even if you are aware of their nature and choose to use them, there are those who chose to do so incompletely.

I once left a public circle, excusing myself, because the participants of this circle brought in three of the four classical elements, leaving the fourth hanging there unacknowledged. Often the reason for doing this is based on elemental magic, where the omission of one element can strengthen the bind of that element to an object. This is not appropriate to a temple rite, however.

While using three, four and even five or eight point temple rites is an excellent way to construct a rite, you must use the entire collection associated with those points. If you are using the classical elements, use all four. If you are using the Eastern elements, use all five. The systems must be used intact and with the understanding of all present.

In short, the use of any entity in temple construction means using the whole of that entity, so know what you're doing and why.

Integrating the Temple Rite into the Ritual:

Another debate in the construction of the temple rite is whether the temple should be integrated into the ritual itself or a distinct and separate rite. As with some of the other aspects of the temple rite, I think this is largely a matter of personal taste. Traditionally, the temple rite may be performed by people newer to the circle than the larger seasonal rite, and I encourage elders to have their experienced students erect the temple at all times, as it is something easily mastered.

In a circle of equals, however, there is little point in dividing up the labor if there is a person who sincerely wishes to integrate the temple rite into a single ritual that includes the temple, the seasonal rite, Cakes and Ale and closing the temple. My only advice in such situations is to strive for something with consistency.

Location of the Elements:

As I touched upon briefly, the location of the elements is a very sincere debate in the Wiccan community. I, personally, prefer air in the North and also starting from the North, but that's because of my training outside of Wicca. Indeed, while I prefer Air in the North, people familiar with *All One Wicca* know that I tend to *teach* the more traditional Air in the East. I'm already blowing people's minds in that book without making them feel that a Wiccan "given" is not actually given at all.

Perhaps the classical essay on the use of air in the North is Mike Nichol's *"Re-thinking the Watchtowers, or thirteen reasons why air should be in the North*[41]*."* For me, the decision is based on experience, more than words, and I encourage readers to experiment and research until they find what works for them.

Permanent or Temporary?

Gardner's assertion that the temple be portable and capable of being set up anywhere was largely based on a flawed view of Wicca as a reconstruction of the religion of Margaret Murray's Witch-Cult. While there are very good reasons for a temporary temple, I personally find that permanent structures are preferable when possible.

In Ceremonial Magic the permanent conjury is a mainstay. If you want your temple to be dual-use, I recommend a permanent structure. If you are just using it for celebratory worship then it can be as temporary or as permanent as you feel comfortable with. To me, it's a non-debate.

Erect the Temple around Participants or let them in?

The last debate in temple construction I will discuss is whether the temple should be raised around the participants or whether the participants should be greeted and let inside the temple. While this is usually decided based on tradition, I prefer to welcome people into the temple when there is a mystery rite (and initiations, dedications, movements within ranks of the tradition, etc.) and to erect the

---

[41] Located here: http://www.geocities.com/Athens/Forum/7280/rethink.html here: http://www.ecauldron.com/rethinking.php and here: http://www.sacred-texts.com/bos/bos089.htm

temple around participants when the ritual is informal, celebratory and/or contains non-Wiccan participants.

I think the welcoming-in is more personal, active and direct, and the erecting around is more passive. There are reasons for the passive circle but the fact remains that the ones whom the temple is erected around are audience members, not full participants. A third option, the collectively raised temple, will be covered in the next chapter.

Chapter Nine: Temples for Formal Worship

Formal worship is defined here as any rite which is pre-planned, follows a set of directions and occurs for a defined reason. Seasonal worship, rites to move within the ranks of a tradition, dedications and initiations are examples of things that may happen in formal worship situations.

While it is possible to use minimalist temples for formal worship and, indeed, they should be used where other temples are not permitted or feasible, these rites are designed as functional examples of rites that work on all five dimensions of erecting the temple when properly performed.

A Formal Temple for Solitary Practice:

While there are three distinct methods for bringing multiple people into the temple, the solitary temple eliminates that problem because the person erecting the temple is the only person there. If you wish to have two to three people in your temple, scale down the group circles rather than scale solitary ones up.

Pre-temple preparation:

I'm going to assume that since you're doing this as a solitary, you know how to properly prepare yourself before the ritual, and since it's a formal one, you'll do so. Some general techniques for purification are included at the end of this work if you lack ideas. At the least, you should be bathed, skyclad or clothed in appropriate ritual garb or clean street clothes and at peace with yourself and your surroundings before attempting the ritual.

This temple rite falls into the general category of tetragram circles, but also contains a mixing of the waters which is a Land-Sea-Sky rite. It is possible to overlay these, as done here, or use only one. In my opinion, this is a good temple for learning these aspects of erecting the temple, but a solid everyday use circle is far shorter.

The Rite:

Lay on the floor and make a mark where your head and the soles of your feet are when you lay straight. Use this measurement to inscribe upon the floor a circle whose diameter is your measure. If you cannot write upon the floor, use rope, tape or small stones to mark out the area. It is possible to purchase bags of cleaned, polished pebbles large enough to place easily and small enough to be useful at most pond supply stores.

Make sure you have all the equipment you will need for the ritual before you lay the last stone, as you will not be crossing the line of stones until the ritual is over, unless there is an emergency. At the center of the circle you should have placed a small round table. The table should be large enough to hold all of your supplies for the whole of the rite. This ritual follows an out-then-in format, which means that the things on the table—your altar—will be removed from the altar, used and returned to the altar. This is different from the four small altar format generally preferred for large group gatherings, in which the candles, tools, etc., may be left at the outer edge of the temple.

At the least, you should have four substantial candles, one to mark each of the elements. While some prefer the cardinal colors of yellow, red, blue and green, I prefer more subtle tones, a sort of sky blue and white marbled appearance for air, opalescent reds and oranges for fire, seafoams and teals for water and rusty browns for earth. It is also possible to use all white candles in this rite, or whatever you have handy. You will need something to light the candles with, and I generally use a small candle which represents the light of my gods and my ancestors. Matches, lighters and any other fire sources are acceptable as well—don't fall into the trap of thinking that tiny ephemera such as how the candles are lit are of particular import. Anyone who has the audacity to tell you that blowing out a candle damages its energy or that one kind of lighter is best probably owns a shop selling candle snuffers and "the right kind" of lighters.

In addition to the candles and their accoutrements, you will need a bell, a mirror, incense (for small spaces I prefer cones or sticks to resins burned on charcoal, less carbon monoxide that way,) rock salt, sea salt, an athamé or other metal implement, a (wooden) wand or other piece of wood and a small dish of rain water.

Begin by clearing your mind and spirit of all negativity. Inhale the flavors of the unlit candles and incense, the pure scent of washed skin, the crispness of clean cloth and perhaps the lingering scent of your ritual equipment. Light the candle for the east[42] and carry it to

---

[42] I *really* do prefer air in the north, but I will go with convention for these rites.

the eastern point of the circle. Hold it aloft (this is why a substantial thick candle is better than a taper here) and with your back to the altar say:

"Before the kindling eastern fire I lift my light that light and air be brought into the temple this night[43]."

Walk once clockwise round the circle, then return to the altar in a straight line. Take up the candle for the South and do as you had with the eastern one:

"Before the warning southern fire I lift my light that warmth and strength be brought into the temple this night."

Circumambulate once again, repeating the technique for the remaining candles, saying the following at the appropriate points:

"Before the dying western fire I lift my light that birth and rebirth be brought into this temple this night."

"Before the glowing northern fire I lift my light that support and friendship be brought into the temple this night."

Return to the center, and speaking to the east from behind the altar say. "Now are the balefires lit, the kin who've gone before and have yet to come awakened."

Hold the mirror so that you can see your reflection. "This is the face of the one who would know the gods this night." Walk around the circle, with the mirror facing inward. As you walk, try to visualize a line of light building around you. "Let nothing remain in this circle that is not pure of heart and intent." Walk around once more, with the mirror facing outward. "Beyond the barrier you stay, all that would do ill."

Set down the mirror, and pick up the incense. Light it or add incense to the coals. "Let this smell be foul for those who'd be with the gods for any reason they'd find objectionable. Let this be a preparing of the way, all that is foul departs, all that is fair remains."

Place the dish of water central to the altar. "This water from the world above washes away all pollution, cleansing and refreshing the world.

Hold rock (earth) salt in each hand. "Salt of the earth purifies or destroys, like the power of the gods. With earth I charge this water of air." Add to water.

---

[43] Or day, I suppose.

Hold sea salt in each hand. "From the waters of life all energy flows, to return again to the womb. With the powers of the sea I charge this water of earth and air."

Dip your right[44] hand into the water. "Of land, sea and sky let the temple be constructed. Strong as a mountain, swift as the sea, changeable as the sky."

Place your right hand to your brow. "May I be worthy of the presence of the gods."

Dip your left hand into the water. "Of land, sea and sky let the temple remain. Long-lived as a mountain, enduring as the sea, ever-present as the sky."

Place your left hand to your heart. "May I know and do their will."

Hold your hands above the water, palms up. "Grant me your presence this night if it be your will."

Walk around the circle, using your right hand to drip water along the boundary. "By land, sea and sky I exhort you." (This may be repeated up to three times, in ascending volume.)

Hold the athamé in your left hand, and the wand in your right. Cross your arms over your torso and feel the energy flowing between the two items. If needed, balance the two so that they are equal in potency. Pass both through the incense. "May these be an extension of myself and my will."

Set the athamé down. Walk around the circle with the wand, balancing it in *both* hands and using it to clean up the boundaries of the circle as needed. "Let this temple sacred be."

Set the wand down and pick up the athamé. Use it to remove the temple from the outer area (walk around again with it.) "Let this temple be a place out of place, a time out of time, a worthy home for those who dwell within."

Set down the athamé. Pick up the bell. Strike it once: "Now is the temple built, welcome all within." Strike it again. "Now is the sacred space decreed." Strike it a third time. "As I will, so mote it be."

Take a moment to feel the temple, patch it as needed, then begin the ritual you built it for.

---

[44] If you are left-handed, you may reverse these, although I do not recommend it.

A Formal Pentagram[45] Temple for Solitary Practice.

Not all formal temples use a lot of tools. The tools are primarily keys to help you unlock parts of the rite you have already prepared within yourself. I strongly recommend learning each of the area cleansing parts of rites like the previous until they become second nature to you.

Preparing the rite:

This rite requires a large piece of durable chalk (I prefer white sidewalk chalk) and a flat writing surface, such as a concrete floor. I don't recommend doing this outside in an urban area where you will be observed, as the symbolism may disturb ignorant neighbors. It is possible to prepare the area ahead of time by using five candles and drawing a circle to encompass the pentagram.

To properly practice this rite, you will need to understand the use of five critical states. For UEWiccans, these are covered in the states conveyed in the first circle discussion of the elemental visualizations, and the second circle discussions of invocation and evocation. For the rest, I will try to describe the sensations in text, but if you're unfamiliar with these concepts, you'll need to practice them before doing this rite. This rite uses energetic, traditional and spiritual and mental aspects over the physical, but if you're crawling on the floor drawing lines the physical gets through to your body just fine.

I will resist the urge to discuss my opinions of Wiccan traditions that do not teach these basic concepts. They are not the manipulation of energy some would claim but they are skills for dealing with data from the outside and inside world. A fully human human, what a member of certain traditions might call a proper person, should have these skills, even if they don't understand what they are.

The Rite Itself:

Prepare a 9ft diameter circle in a clean, open space. Clean the area with seawater and hyssop or the purification techniques of your preference, using a broom if you use one regularly. If you do use it, sweep outward, as you wish to create a place that is devoid of exter-

---

[45] Drawn five-sided figure.

nal energy. Remember that traditionally one sweeps inward to keep energy inside, but this is a rite that works best with a blank slate.[46]

If you are using candles, I recommend lighting them at the start of the rite, not as you reach each point. If you are using tools in your later ritual, I recommend using a flat pentacle (such as one carved of wax or clay) to hold the tools at the center. If you are fortunate enough to have a packed earth place to do this rite, you can also use the athamé to draw the lines.

Stand at north[47] (1) and call to mind the triumph of spirit over will. Invoke your patron deity (your dominant one if you have one) that your will and theirs be one.

When you have established a connection, move to point 2, drawing a line.

At point 2, ground yourself. Send your energy down (in UEW, connect with the element earth) and root it into place so that you are firmly established in terms of power over self. When you have established a connection, move to point 3, drawing a line.

Repeat the procedure at 3 (self over others, in UEW the element of fire and/or air directed internally) and 4 (others over self, in UEW the element of fire and/or air directed externally.)

At 5, evoke the state of power/will over self. In UEW, this is largely understood as the element of water, or the womb visualization, it is very much about the universe supporting and assisting you. Return to 1. Center then evoke until the invocation and evocation are of equal power with the other energies you've brought to bear.

The temple is complete, so begin the rest of the ritual.

A Formal Group Temple featuring "Welcoming in."

There are three ways to place members of a coven or other working group into a temple rite, they can be welcomed, they can erect the temple as a co-operative rite or they can have the temple cast around them. I prefer the act of welcoming the coveners when doing initiation rites, rites involving other mysteries and movement within the coven ranks because you can use the opportunity of wel-

---

[46] Unless you're doing it in a permanent pentagram.
[47] This should be determined with a compass. If south has a stronger magnetic pull where you are, you should start at the south and move clockwise from that point. I do not recommend that you go counterclockwise except at times such as November Eve where you may do it intentionally.

coming in to ask if each fulfills the duty of their membership. This is even sometimes done at sword point, but I don't recommend that unless *everyone* involved understands the meaning and the reasoning behind that.

Our sample welcoming in temple rite expects that you have a better understanding of the tetragram circle than other forms, and is therefore presented in a condensed format for ease of use. You will need an athamé, a lit taper, anointing oil[48], blessed salt water (charged in a chalice with an athamé before or during the rite,) incense that can be moved[49], four earthenware containers holding pure water and floating candles, a goblet of wine, a small table at each quarter point and a small central altar.

Begin by marking out the circle where the temple is to be erected. Place tables at each quarter point and the altar at the center. Prepare any tools that are not ready for the rite. Place containers of water with candles on each of the four tables[50]. Circumambulate with lit incense and sprinkling empowered water, saying "With Fire and Air/Water and Earth I remove everything from this space that is not fit to stand before the gods with open eyes and head held high."

Using the lit taper, move to each of the four candles, lighting them "earth surrounds, water supports, fire consumes and air is consumed."

At Air, recall the elemental state of air[51], bring the element of air into the temple by breathing out and manifesting air. Raise your hands above your head, palms up and manifest air as spirit. Drag spirit into the circle with your hands and circumambulate once more.

At Fire, recall the elemental state of fire by focusing inward. Place the hands on the heart, palms inward, and manifest fire and strength and physicality. Drag them into the circle with your hands and circumambulate once more.

---

[48] See glossary.
[49] Hanging censer, bundle of herbs or even a stick.
[50] Essentially, each of these markers is all four elements and none, so there is no conflict between any energies or symbolism. The earth surrounds, the water supports, the fire consumes and the air is consumed.
[51] If you practice UEW, these are discussed *ad nauseam* in the elemental visualizations.

At Water and Earth repeat the actions, with the palms upwards and out forward to accept water's support, and the palms downwards and at the sides to accept earth's stability. Use the mental images of the elemental states to move each into the circle.

Welcome in the gods of your group and of your ancestors. Share a libation with them. A votive sacrifice, such as that of herbs on the fire, is appropriate here. Complete the circle in accordance with your tradition.

Using the athamé, cut a hole in the pattern of energies at the east[52] of the circle. Welcome each member in one at a time. Ask if they come into the temple in perfect love and perfect trust, but not if that's a concept they do not understand! Purify them with smoke, water, energy and a solar cross or pentagram on the forehead. The last part should be a kiss and/or hug as equals before the gods.

Once each member has been welcomed, retrace the cut and restore the energies, closing it with a sealing pentagram.

A Temple Rite Cast Around a Coven:

The previous rite assumed a familiarity with a number of concepts, but this one should be capable of being cast with a minimum of advanced understanding. I don't recommend this version for rituals expecting a great deal of tightness when raising energy, but it is a very easy functional circle.

Assemble the group in a circle. Have them clasp hands and take two steps back to make an effective distance between them. Break hands. The leader, if leading an inexperienced group or a group with newcomers, should take this time to explain what the temple rite is. Ask people who are not prepared to face the gods at this time to leave. Reinforce the fact that there is no shame in doing so. If you have too much going on to face them wholeheartedly, you should not be engaging in worship as a group without working through your stuff. It's honest and brave to admit this.

The leader should stand at the east and light a yellow candle. "The east is the source of beginnings, of sunrises and births. Its element is air, its color is yellow, its lesson is creativity, and its people are our descendants, flowing out from ourselves in love and hope.

---

[52] The actual use of east here is not a big deal. This can be done anywhere, although east (entrances) is preferable to west (exits).

Here I bring light to the east, that we recognize the power of air. May we be like this element, creative, eternal, with an invisible but undeniable strength. Let all our descendants yet to come look back on this day as one when we stood as one, worthy of the gods."

The leader should walk around the circle clockwise once, carrying the candle. He will repeat this at each compass point. Incense is lit. The leader lustrates (passes the incense over and around) the person to his right (facing inward.) "Begone all ill-health, all ill thought. Welcome to this circle in peace." He may then either lustrate the next or allow the members of the group to each do so for their neighbor.

At the south, the leader lights a red candle. "The south is the double edged sword, bringing warmth and gentle breezes and disease and thunder. Its element is fire, its color is red, its lesson is that no tale has but one side and its people are our peers, those who'd do us good and those who'd do us ill. Here I bring light to the south, that we recognize the power of fire. May we be like this element, tempering and strong. May our destructive powers mingle with our constructive for the good of the all. Let all our peers know those in this temple stand as one, worthy of the gods.

The leader hands each member of the group a candle, and lights them, clockwise. As each candle is lit, the one holding it is told "Let this fire kindle your strengths and burn away all your weaknesses. Welcome to this circle in strength."

At the west, the leader lights a blue candle. "The west is the ultimate destination, path to the underworld, where the sun retreats at night. Its element is water, its color is blue, its lesson that where we come from is where we end up and it is for that reason that its people are our ancestors, those who wait and watch as we go where they have gone before. Here I bring light to the west, that we recognize the power of water. Water that supports and gives life but also can take it away. May we never forget where we came from. Let all our ancestors look upon those in this temple with pride, and know they are worthy of the gods."

A dish of seawater is raised. "The creative and destructive powers of fire and water are humankind's right to control. Here we quench our tempering fire that the blessings and strengths of fire and water be upon us."

Each of the candles passed around earlier is extinguished in the dish. As each flame goes out, the leader or person holding the dish says "From water we are born, to water we return."

The candles are gathered[53], and the leader moves on to the north. He lights a green candle. "The north is the strong hand that touches the weak with love. Its element is earth, its color is green, its lesson is that we learn as much from teaching as from our teachers and it is for that reason that its people are our teachers. Here I bring light to the north, that we recognize the foundation that is earth. Earth which nurtures and grounds so that we may reach for the stars without falling. May we reach the point where we are always worthy of the gods."

The leader stands before the group. "My name is Mark[54], I stand before you as the leader of Parnassus Coven. I bring you my light and love. I hope to be worthy of your love and trust and worthy of the gods."

The person to his immediate left speaks next. "My name is Joe, I stand before you as a member of Parnassus Coven. I bring you my trust and honesty. I hope to be worthy of your love and trust and worthy of the gods."

The next person continues. "My name is Caitlin. I stand before you as a guest of Parnassus Coven. I bring you my open mind. I hope to be worthy of your love and trust and worthy of the gods."

So forth around the circle. When it gets back to the leader, he says "Lord and Lady[55], if it be your will, join us this night as we join with the others of Wicca in your honest worship. If you will not attend, look down firm in the knowledge we do what we do in love and honor and the hope of being worthy."

To the group he says. "Now is the temple complete. May what transpires within these walls of will be all for good and naught for ill."

With the temple erected, begin the ritual. If this temple rite is being used for a group of mixed levels of experience in Wicca, make

---

[53] These candles are not extinguished when this temple is used for February Eve. Instead, each person touches the water and says the same thing.
[54] This is example text.
[55] Ideally, these are the names of the gods of the group.

sure that newcomers and guests have at least a mentor who is willing to answer questions about the rite.

A Co-operative Temple Rite:

Not all covens are strict hierarchies with a well-defined leadership. Many covens are covens of equals, covens in which all members share a basic level of knowledge, whether as beginners in a study group or elders meeting by choice. In these groups, erecting the temple may be assigned to a volunteer, done on a rotating basis or done in the form of co-operative rites.

The co-operative rite discussed in this section was prepared by a working coven of six elders in a singular tradition. In this circle, they chose to use the classical elements of the middle-modern Wicca tetragram circle, but instead of one person calling each of the elements, the group decided that one person, each, would call the four classical elements and the group's shared god and goddess, respectively.

This is not an uncommon practice, but I do not recommend it for beginners, as newcomers regularly get this idea that every Wiccan *is* an element, and that "finding their element," is a sensical concept in Wicca. It is not.

Ideally, if you are using the classical elements, or the neo-classical elements (the four plus a fifth,) you balance all of the elements within yourself. I cannot express my dissatisfaction at new Wiccans who ask the rest of us how to find their element. You do not have an element, you *should* have them all. A preference for one element or the other should not be the deciding factor in who calls what. It would be better in that instance to draw names from a hat than go with a lack of balance.

If randomness is inappropriate, preference should be based instead on the location of the caster's demesnes, with the one with the northernmost home and association at the north of the circle, etc. Since this was a circle of elders, the calls were based on the location of the covenstead. Only after other associations are ruled impossible should elemental correspondences be considered, but bear in mind that using a person who is over-reliant upon an element can unbalance the circle.

Assuming that you've worked out a reasonable distribution, this temple rite uses the concept of "speaker for the east" (and other directions) and "speakers for the gods". This means that the person who takes that part in the temple rite is responsible for the spiritual, traditional, energetic, mental and physical dimensions associated with each of these aspects of the rite.

As an example, the speaker of the east stands at the east and brings in the element of air, the sense of beginnings and sunrises, exploration and creativity. He might say something about the gods and himself, such as "I am Dave of the Covenstead of Mirabilis, I am the speaker for the east. To this circle I bring air and light, that we see our path clearly." He should then do some sort of votive sacrifice affiliated with air, such as burning incense or herbs. He should bring in the element energetically as well, filling the circle with the metaphysical element of air.

The Speaker for the Lord and Lady should enact the blessing of the waters, at the least. Ideally, the positions filled in the erecting of the temple persist through the entire ritual. When I last was witness to a rite quite similar to this, all the quarters were announced simultaneously. It was really quite beautiful. It's also powerful to overlap words, as the Arising Coven ritual later in this book does. Since the words of the speakers must be personalized, however, making overlapping words may require more preparation than they are worth.

Chapter Ten: Closing the Temple

If erecting the temple should be less than 30% of the time spent in the rite, closing or tearing down the temple should be less than half of that. Energetically, the temple begins to collapse when any fragment of the temple is removed. This, not fear of extra-spatial beings, is why leaving the temple during the rite is frowned upon.

A well crafted temporary temple comes down as swiftly as if it were a Roman arch bridge when you remove the keystone. Until and unless you release it, it will not fall. When you release it, it collapses at once. Finding this energetic keystone is really a matter of practice, but it can be accomplished swiftly by puncturing the cone of power and releasing it in a directed manner or otherwise abruptly ending. If you have experienced the common technique of going through the motions of deconstructing a circle after it has very clearly dissolved, you'll know that it can be very silly to carefully "reabsorb the energy into your athamé," when you're already sent every free ounce away.

Since we've examined the temple rite as preparing the way for communion with the divine, ending the rite is not ending that communion, which should've happened in the ritual, but instead, the closing rite is acknowledging that the communion occurred, and preparing yourself to return to the normal and mundane world outside of the direct attention of the gods. In general the closing rite should be based on the temple rite itself. If you used the elemental quarters, acknowledge them leaving and in your life after the ritual (i.e.: "May we now take air and its lessons forward in our lives until we meet again.") If you welcomed the gods, thank them appropriately.

In general, if you can write a list of the steps you used in the erection of the temple, you merely undo them in the reverse, so that the last step in creating the space becomes the first step in expelling it. It is not necessary to do this counterclockwise, although some may prefer to do so. The point of the rite is to provide closure to the ritual and make sure everything is accomplished before moving out of the ritual space. As such, it is an afterthought *by definition.*

If I, personally, am using an elemental tetragram circle for my temple rite, I generally dismiss it with the Arising Coven rite given in *All One Wicca*:

Leader: "We met this day/night in love and peace, and our rite was blessed by the light of all within this circle. May the goodness, energy and light within be reflected in our lives without. Blessed be the Lord and Lady, in all the ways they were reflected tonight, as hope, as promise, as healing and as the sacred mother and father to whom we owe our existence."

East: "From the east we were granted air, and the first rays of the sun, from the east came light, and from there it shall return." (snuff candle)

South: "Holy fire from the south cleansed and tempered us, to there let the fires return. " (snuff)

West: "Water that is life, brought from the west to nurture, cleanse and uplift, to the west return." (snuff)

North: "Earth, from which we came, housed in the north, to the north return." (snuff)

Leader: "Lord and Lady, sacred parents, sacred lovers, sacred children, may your light grow ever stronger, lifted into the heavens as moon and sun, and reflected in the eyes of all who can gaze skyward with the light of the Law within them." (candles snuffed)

"Now is our rite complete. May the circle be open, but ever unbroken!"

Chapter Eleven: When to not use the Temple

The erecting the temple rite is probably the one rite in a Wiccan's toolbox that he or she should be so fluent in that doing it in multiple forms and multiple scenarios should be second nature. A well-schooled Wiccan should have at least four temple rites memorized, including at least one outside the elemental tetragram family, and, in addition, should have enough knowledge of the general class of rites to come up with one on the fly as the circumstances warrant.

While the inclusion of minimalist circles in this work can be taken to mean that I encourage using those small rites in situations where they will fit, the long and short of it is that you should never be using a temple rite, in any form, where you are not preparing the way for communion with the divine.

If, for example, you are "casting spells" or doing divination that is not about the gods, you probably should not be erecting a temple. Likewise, you needn't erect a temple for simple one-way communication with the gods, such as most prayers and low-level energy requests. "Preparing the way," should be a mantra. If there is no way to prepare, it's not time for the temple rite.

You should not use the Wiccan temple rite for Ceremonial Magic, unless the rite is specifically dual-use. You should not use a dual-use rite without understanding how it works on all levels. You certainly should not create an air-tight ceremonial circle if your intention is to direct energy outward.

Lastly you should use absolutely no temple rite that you do not understand the entirety of. If the rite invokes watchers, unnamed gods, dread lords, energies, elementals, totemic spirits, ancestors and anything else that you do not have a coherent and in-depth understanding of, do not do it as written. If you stumble upon words in a temple rite that you don't know, find them out before going ANY further. Do not, under any circumstances, invoke, exhort, exorcise, banish, call, converse with or wish upon anything that you do not know the nature of. It is unlikely that you could cause harm in that way, but you could certainly give offense, which is the opposite of what a temple rite is designed to do.

Ask yourself, with all such rites, if the job of this rite is to prepare the way for communion with the divine. Once you've decided your ritual does that, assess your plans and ask the following questions:

- Does my planned ritual require the removal of negative energy, spiritual pollution or other such concepts before doing it? Have I done so or does the rite do so?
- Do I need to invoke the power of repetition and the power of numbers by performing traditional techniques or using time-honored methods?
- Am I prepared, mentally, spiritually, physically, traditionally and energetically to do this at this time and in this place? If not, will the rite make me so?
- Does this ritual give no offense and take only what is mine to take?
- Do I know what I am doing and why?
- Is it coherent and sensical?
- Is it right with the gods, my ancestors and others whom I do not wish to offend?
- Will the temple rite hold or release the energies, if any, that are generated in the rite in an appropriate manner?
- Am I erecting the temple because someone said to or for a *real* reason?
- If I imagined that I had a finite number of temples to erect in my life would this seem like a wasted one?
- Once again, *does this rite require or create communion with the divine?*

Using these questions, it should be quite easy to assess whether you should erect a temple for your purpose or not. Practice, experience and trial and error will help you come to know what is needed every time. Understanding the *why* will give you the *how*, but that rarely works the other way around.

Hopefully I've given you the why of the temple. It's up to you to find the how.

General Purification Techniques

Most purification techniques are focused upon using the physical cleansing of the body to encourage the spiritual cleansing of the spirit. The addition of specific things to your bathwater and/or soap is supposed to assist in different ways, but you can use the same mental imagery to assist in the purification, regardless of the ingredients you have added. They are listed in the order of my personal preference for these things.

For a literal purification procedure, visualize the negativity washing down into the drain as you bath or shower. When you are done, anoint yourself at the wrists, heart and forehead with clary sage, monarda, peppermint, labdanum or dragon's blood. These latter two should be in a very small amounts in a carrier oil, such as evening primrose.

It is also possible to wash the hands and face in a basin using the principle of sympathy. You should use clean, natural colored cotton cloth to dry with. It is possible to wash the faces and hands of coveners, and it can be a beautiful, if damp, experience.

Ingredients to add to Soap and Bathwater:

Monarda (Bee Balm) and Eucalyptus: Helps to open the mind to subtle sensations. The monarda can be replaced with a true mint or lemon balm.

Salt: Grounds, centers, and disinfects but can be very drying on the skin. You can use iron, zinc or silver oxides (in the form of calamine powder, for example,) to balance the harshness of the salt.

Honey: Used with or without milk, it does many of the same things as salt without causing distress to the skin.

Rose Otto: Expensive, but excellent as a mental cue.

Night Blooming Jasmine or Moonflower: Helps to bring the nocturnal into the day.

Hyssop and Sea Water: I generally reserve this for when I've had to deal with physical death.

Holy Water: Any consecrated water can be added to a bath to add the properties of the water to the bathwater, although the waters obviously need to be appropriate for your ends.

Dry Cleansing Methods:

If a bath is inappropriate (you're working with a god of arid lands, for example) there are three major ways of doing cleansing that may be more appropriate. You can use alcohol, such as high-purity food-grade ethanol, to make a tincture of sacred herbs, and rather than visualize the alcohol running down the drain, imagine it evaporating. You can also use a combination of ground sacred stones and herbs to scrub the skin, although this can get expensive and time-consuming.

The last, and perhaps easiest, of these methods is lustration, the act of walking through sacred smoke. This is simple enough that it can be added to any of the techniques discussed above, as well as used on its own.

General Mental Preparedness Techniques

The easiest mental preparedness technique to describe is deity-focused centering prayer. Close your eyes and inhale, and as you exhale call your deity's name (or one of them) inside of your head. Breathe deeply and with intention and think of the meaning of your relationship with your god. As your mind strays, return to the name of your god until your mind does not stray anymore. At that point, enjoy some silence and then you should be in the right mindset for your ritual.

More complicated is to lay flat and attempt to move only one voluntary muscle at a time. The concentration that this can result in can be used to move involuntary muscles as well, and this technique, while time-consuming, is still worth pursuing.

If that's still not your speed, you can try a static meditation, like most yoga, or a dynamic one like Tai Chi. All of these can result in increased mental preparedness, as can the focus brought on my playing an instrument or dancing. John Dee used the construction of complex geometric figures as a way of preparing to receive angels and my own experiences with that show that it certainly changes something inside the brain.

Exercises designed to stimulate creativity, brainstorming and idea generation can also assist in mental preparedness, but unlike purification techniques these can easily become a crutch when overused. Every technique needs moderation.

Four Additional Erecting the Temple Rites

The following erecting the temple rites each represent an important variation on erecting the temple for the context of this book. They are provided primarily as examples.

Gardnerian[56]:

Early Gardnerian (1949):

It is most convenient to mark the circle with chalk, paint or otherwise, to show where it is; but marks on the carpet may be utilized. Furniture may be placed to indicate the bounds. The only circle that matters is the one drawn before every ceremony with either a duly consecrated Magic Sword or an Athamé. The circle is usually nine feet in diameter, unless made for some very special purpose. There are two outer circles, each six inches apart, so the third circle has a diameter of eleven feet.

Having chosen a place proper, take the sickle or scimitar of Art or a Witch's Athamé, if thou mayest obtain it, and stick it into the center, then take a cord, and 'twere well to use the Cable Tow for this, and loop it over the Instrument, four and one half feet, and so trace out the circumference of the circle, which must be traced either with the Sword, or the knife with the black hilt, or it be of little avail, but ever leave open a door towards the North. Make in all 3 circles, one within the other , and write names of power between these.

First draw circle with Magic Sword or Athamé.

Consecrate Salt and Water: Touch water with Athamé, saying, "I exorcise thee, O creature of Water, that thou cast out from Thee all the impurities and uncleannesses of the Spirits of the World of Phantasm, so they may harm me not, in the names of Aradia and Cernunnos."

Touching Salt with Athamé, say, "The Blessings of Aradia and Cernunnos be upon this creature of Salt, and let all malignity and hindrance be cast forth hencefrom, and let all good enter herein, for without Thee man cannot live, wherefore I bless thee and invoke thee, that thou mayest aid me."

Then put the Salt into the water.

Sprinkle with exorcised water.

---

[56] Note that the only Gardnerian rituals contained herein are identical to the Aiden Kelley collection, available online, and therefore do not violate any oaths or copyrights.

> *Light candles; say, "I exorcise thee, O Creature of Fire, that every kind of Phantasm may retire from thee, and be unable to harm or deceive in any way, in the names of Aradia and Cernunnos."*
>
> *Caution initiate (if any); warn companions; enter circle and close doors with 3 pentagrams.*
>
> *Proclaim object of working*
>
> *Circumambulate 3 times or more before commencing work.*
>
> *Summon: "I summon, stir, and Call thee up, thou Mighty Ones of the East, South, West, and North." Salute and draw pentacle with Magic Sword or Athamé, the first stroke being from the top down to the left.*

Later Gardnerian (1957):

> *All Are Purified*
>
> *Magus consecrates salt and water.*
>
> *High Priestess kneels at Altar, takes up Sword, says, "I conjure thee, O Sword of Steel, to serve me as a defence in all Magical Operations. Guard me at all times against mine enemies, both visible and invisible. Grant that I may obtain what I desire in all things wherein I may use Thee, Wherefore do I bless Thee and invoke Thee in the names of Aradia and Cernunnos." Gives Sword to Magus.*
>
> *Magus kneeling hands her vessel of consecrated Water and Aspergillum. He Casts the circle, three circles, on the lines marked out, starting at the East and returning to the East. High Priestess follows, Asperging circle (sprinkling it to purify it) and all present and finally herself. Then she goes round again censing it. (Everyone in the circle must be sprinkled and censed.)*
>
> *She walks slowly round circle, saying, "I conjure Thee, O circle of Space, that thou be a Boundary and a Protection and a meeting place between the world of Men and that of the Dread Lords of the Outer Spaces, that Thou be cleansed, Purified, and strengthened to be a*
>
> *Guardian and a Protection that shall preserve and contain That Power which we so earnestly desire to raise within thy bounds this night, wherefore do I bless thee and entreat thee to aid me in the endeavor, in the names of Aradia and Cernunnos."*
>
> *Magus then summons the Mighty Ones as usual.*
>
> *High Priestess stands in front of Altar. High Priestess assumes Goddess position (arms crossed). Magus kneeling in front of her, draws pentacle on her body with Phallus-headed Wand, Invokes (Drawing down the Moon), "I Invoke and beseech Thee, O mighty Mother of all life and fertility. 'By seed and root, by stem and bud, by leaf and flower and fruit, by Life and Love, do I invoke Thee' to descend into the body*

of thy servant and High Priestess (name)." (The Moon having been drawn down, i.e., link established, Magus and all male officers give fivefold kiss; all others bow.)

High Priestess in Goddess position says, arms crossed,

"Mother, Darksome and Divine, Mine the Scourge and Mine the Kiss, The Five-point Star of Love and Bliss; Here I charge ye in this Sign. (Opens out Arms to pentacle position)

Bow before my Spirit bright (All bow) Aphrodite, Arianrhod, Lover of the Horned God, Queen of Witchery and Night.

Diana, Brigid, Melusine, Am I named of old by men, Artemis and Cerridwen, Hell's dark mistress, Heaven's Queen.

Ye who ask of me a boon, Meet ye in some hidden shade, Lead my dance in greenwood glade by the light of the full moon.

Dance about mine altar stone, Work my holy magistry, ye who are fain of sorcery, I bring ye secrets yet unknown.

No more shall ye know slavery who tread my round the Sabbat night. Come ye all naked to the rite in sign that ye are truly free.

Keep ye my mysteries in mirth, Heart joined to heart and lip to lip. Five are the points of fellowship that bring ye ecstasy on Earth.

No other law but love I know; by naught but love may I be known, and all that liveth is my own: From me they come, to me they go.

Universal Eclectic Wicca:

Solitary[57]:

Casting the circle: Caster places white or appropriately colored candles at the compass points, the altar is at the center of the circle. Upon the altar are a small white or beeswax candle, two larger candles, the censer with unlit incense, the athamé, a dish of salt, a goblet of water, small cakes or cookies for "cakes and ale," a goblet of wine, an offering dish and any items for work to be done within the cast circle. The caster takes a short moment, eyes closed, to become "at peace" before standing before the altar. The small candle is lit, and the caster walks toward the east.

He[58] lights the yellow or white candle from the small candle, saying "Here I call forth the powers of air from the east, that I may be like the air, unfettered and pure."

He takes a moment to remember the air visualization, and to contemplate the meaning of the east, air and freedom before continuing onward.

---

[57] From *All One Wicca*.
[58] Or "she." He is meant in its sense as gender neutral.

He lights the red or white candle to the south with the small candle saying. "Here I call forth the powers of fire from the south, that I may be like fire, enduring all hardships to become strengthened."

Here the caster recalls his own "trials by fire" and contemplates the possibility of more, the meaning of the words spoken is thought on, and the caster continues.

He lights the blue or white candle to the west, saying, "Here I call forth the powers of water, that I may be like water, supporting and protecting all that I encounter." Here the caster contemplates the water visualization and the meaning of the west in his life.

He moves on to the north, lighting the green or white candle. "Here I call forth the power of Earth, that I may be like earth, grounded at all times." Here, the caster grounds and thinks before moving to the east to say: "Welcome Air, Fire, Water, Earth, shine your light and lend your strength to this my circle tonight/today."

Still moving clockwise, the caster returns to the altar, and lights incense saying. "Negative forces begone, you are not welcome here." He breathes deeply of the incense and banishes away negative forces within before circling clockwise thrice with the censer, visualizing hate, jealousy and the like fleeing from the smoke.

He returns to the altar, picks up the athamé and picks up a measure of salt with its tip. Inserting the tip of the blade into the water he says "As man to woman so blade to chalice, I purify this water with love, light and power." The caster then walks around the circle, sprinkling the salted water about the circle thrice. Returning to the altar, he raises the athamé to the sky and visualizes a beam of blue light filling it, then walks once around the circle, using the blade and its light to "cut" a space between the worlds. This done, he moves to the altar and lights the two candles. "Lord and Lady, I invite you to this my worship, that you may look upon my devotions and celebrations and be heartened and strengthened by them." The caster turns toward the west and announces. "Now is my circle cast, unbreakable and without harm. Thus is sacred space decreed, and no act goes unnoticed. So mote it be."

Arising Coven:

This ritual begins with the entire group standing in a circle, a small fire or candle is burning on the altar. There should be at least four people, plus a coven leader. A bell is rung three times by the leader at the altar. (S)he lights the solar candle from the altar flame. "Kindle this flame from the fire of the Sun, the bell has been rung, the circle begun." (At the Community a flame would be lit from the first rays of the sun and kept burning until the ritual took place that evening, although "like" easily replaces "from.") The coven leader then holds the flame eastward.

"First in the East, so to the East we are first, lighting the flame like the sun lights the Earth." The candle is passed to a person who stands at the East, this person should be a very "air" aligned person, or anyone who feels drawn that way. The East person lights the yellow candle, saying something about the East, the air, the sunrise, or whatever, ending with "so mote it be," repeated by the coven. (We refrain from the use of defined statements because they may become meaningless with repetition.)

The leader then takes the lighter candle from them and walks clockwise, reaching the south, (s)he hands the lighter candle to the quarter guard there, saying. "Fire of Fires, far to the south, the Fire is bright, light casts away doubt." The quarter guard makes his/her statement, and then the leader brings the flame to the west.

"Ocean, Sea, River, Pond, lake stream and brook, everflowing be the water, first home that we took." (This represents the Silver Chalice Community's strong sense of evolutionary science, and may be changed if found offensive for some reason.) The quarter guard speaks ending with "so mote it be," and is echoed, and the leader continues.

"Grounded in Earth, we rose to touch the air, Blessed be the Earth, sacred Mother, ever fair. " The quarter guard says his/her thing, then the priestess walks clockwise to the altar, holding the lighter candle aloft.

(S)he raises the solar candle and that which represents the moon. "As the Sun lights the moon, so light, that the heavens shine" and lights the lunar candle, facing East. The two candles are set down in holders, next to two unlit candles representing the God and Goddess. The Censer, which sits to the east next to the quarter candle is held up by the quarter guard of the East while the quarter guard of the South holds up a small dry branch lit from the South candle. This firebrand is called "the sacred wand." At the same time, the quarter guard of the West holds up a goblet of water and the guard of the North holds up a dish of salt. The following two sections are performed in synch and, timed correctly, are beautiful expressions.

East-South	West-North
East "As the sun lights the south and greets the east.	West "As the west waters come and meet the north
A union, a bond is formed united, in love, the fire meets the air	A gath'ring, a bond is formed As one, together this salt, this water
(The incense is raised to the	(three measures of salt are

down pointed firebrand encasing it. As the incense lights, the firebrand is quenched)	added to the water on the point of an athamé.)
Air into fire	Earth into water
Woman to Man	Man to Woman
That all may be joined	That all may be joined
One with the Earth…	
	…One with the Air…
…One with the Water…	
	…One with the Fire.
In love and worship in this circle tonight.	In love and worship in this circle tonight.
South: Now in love, welcome All who would join our circle in love…	North: Now in love, welcome.
	…in light…
… in truth…	…in harmony.
Welcome Lord and Lady, Witness our revels, our worship, our love.	Welcome Goddess and God! And watch over our circle tonight.
With purest air, we welcome you! (South walks around the circle thrice, censing the air. When finished, the censer is laid on the altar and North begins.)	
	With purest water, we welcome you! (North sprinkles the salted water about the circle thrice…)

The tools are placed on the altar and the priestess lights the God and Goddess candles from the lunar/solar ones. "Welcome great ones, who would hear us this fine night, now we begin the change, the alteration of this space, may all who stand purified within who feel in their heart that they cannot worship within feel free to leave." A moment of space, then the coven sword or athamé is lifted from the altar. The leader walks around from the East, behind the ring of coveners, but within the ring of candles (s)he points the coven sword at the floor, and walks around clockwise once, forming a line just beyond the candles. Once (s)he returns to the East, she faces westward, within the circle. "Abandon your negative energies, let them burn into the pure air of the circle, Pain Begone! Hatred Begone! Fear Begone! Only love is Welcome here!"

She travels around once more, again stopping at the East. "Welcome the positive, love, light and peace, breathe in the light, banish the *darkness!"* She travels once more, stopping at the east and walking forward to the altar. Laying down the sword, she steps into the circle, where all join hands. *"Blessed are all who inhabit this space, in welcome, in love, in light, in truth, I speak the words of those who have gone before, 'Let peace reign supreme, unity, strength and Love in The All, Our Selves, our Gods be blessed, for here is our temple, our church and sacred site, here is the foundation upon which we build our rites.' Welcome friends, spirits, gods, those who were, are and will be, feel freedom within and love, The one rule is the one law[59], and by it, all Will be done, The circle is based on Love all, Harm none!"* Each person in the circle says *"Welcome"* to whoever they wish to include, a patron God, a loved one, a spirit, one at a time clockwise, ending with the leader, who welcomes and then says *"By the strength and love of all within, this circle is cast, this rite may begin...So mote it be!"* The coven repeats *"So mote it be!"*

---

[59] This ritual speaks to a more mature understanding of both The Rede and Thelema than that which is discussed within this book, but nonetheless this ritual is a good example ritual to build upon regardless of your skill level.

Glossary

While no means comprehensive, this list defines some of the topics touched upon in this work which are not covered in depth here, but in other works of mine. Most of the words have multiple definitions, and this list only contains the definitions as they appear within this context.

Anointing Oil: Any oil consecrated to the gods and blessed appropriately in ritual used (in this context) to indicate purity and willingness to enter the temple in perfect love and perfect trust. A perfectly functional anointing oil can be made by coating a bay leaf with labdanum resin and allowing the leaf to steep for 2-3 months (in sunlight) in olive oil. I also like combinations of evening primrose and rose otto for this, but they can be pricy. They should be charged in accordance with your tradition.

Casting the Circle: Essentially, erecting the temple.

Charge of The Goddess: An exhortation to She-of-Many-Names written by Doreen Valiente.

Drawing Down the Moon: A rite involving the invocation of She-of-Many-Names or the Primal Initiatrix into the priestess; also the title of Margot Adler's 1979 study into Pagan traditions in the United States.

Erecting the Temple: Constructing an Energetic, Mental, Physical, Spiritual and Traditional space in which to commune with the divine.

Extrapersonal: Literally, that which exists outside the personal (self) alone, and is out of the control of the self.

Extraspatial: Literally, that which exists outside of physical space.

Fivefold Kiss: Ritual element of welcome in the traditional temple rite or shortly thereafter. Source of the phrase "Blessed Be."

Guestright: The ritual obligation to strangers and guests in traditional Hellenic, Germanic and Judaic cultures, as well as others. In short, a guest and his host have a set of responsibilities that must be borne out. Both Zeus and the Abrahamic god allegedly destroy cultures, cities and individuals who violate guestright too strongly. Also called Xenia, Guest-Host Obligation and Guestrite.

Holisticism: The practice of incorporating all the aspects of a thing into the thing. Thus holistic temples use all of the five dimensions of the temple.

Liminality of Man: Humankind's position as a unique creature that is not really an animal or a god but has characteristics of both.

Noble Eightfold Path: In Zen, the practice of Right View, Right Intention, Right Speech, Right Action, Right Livelihood, Right Effort, Right Mindfulness and Right Consciousness.

Officiate: To run a rite or ritual, also one who does such. Also *caster* or *leader*.

Primal Initatrix: See *She-of-Many-Names*.

She-of-Many-Names: Within the mystery traditions of Wicca, she of many names is many goddesses, but not all goddesses. She-of-Many-Names has no singular public name, but is generally accepted to be a Mediterranean goddess of sexuality and female empowerment, including Astarte, Venus and Aphrodite, but not similar goddesses like Juno or Athena. Also called the Primal Initiatrix (she who founds new mysteries.) Some Wiccans also see the concept of Primal Initatrix as a title for many different goddesses who are involved in the action of revealing the mysteries of sex, sexuality and reproduction to adults. Also called *Somn*.

Tetragram Circle: Magical circle or erecting the temple rite based on a set of fours, such as the classical elements, quarters or the Tetragrammaton. Also called elemental tetragram circle.

Triarchy of Man: The idea, prevalent in Classical Mythology, that Humankind is essentially three parts, the part like a god, the part like an animal and a third, liminal part that is neither like a god nor like an animal. See also *Liminality of Man*.

Votive Sacrifice: A small gift to the gods in fulfillment of a vow. Traditionally these include burning herbs or the parts of food animals not used for food, the burial or dropping into wells and swift rivers of money and charms. A votive candle is a hold-over from a time when candles were not particularly cheap and burning a candle for a deity alone, not for light or heat, was a sacrifice of money or time.

Will: The empowered and self-directed combination of desire, determination and personal planning that directs intent at the individual level. In Greek, Thelema.

Introduction to Bonus Material

As I edited this work, I came to the realization that the Ritual of the Compass Rose and the elemental visualizations are probably required for the non-UEW Wiccans who read this book. If you've really only seen the circle in the distinct elemental tetragram, switching to a new format is not something you're going to be able to do without some more examples. I have provided three herein.

Rather than re-edit these bonus pieces for a new audience, I decided to keep the original text, despite them being available elsewhere. Please understand, however, that much of *The Compass Rose* is quoted in this work, so it may be seen as repetitive if read as part of this work, not as a distinct piece of material. It was always my intention that this work be able to be used as a stand-alone book, and this bonus material is provided to help aid that cause.

Nonetheless, you must understand the context of each of these pieces of material.

The Ritual of the Compass Rose was created for an audience that wished a ceremonial magic valid alternative to the elemental tetragram. It is not a UEW rite, but may require an advanced understanding of Wicca and/or magic to be fully understood.

The Elemental Visualizations are a part of the UEW curriculum and teach each student the techniques of visualization as well as the four necessary metaphysical states for magic, although they are not taught as those metaphysical states in UEW.

The Heraldic Circle was serialized in the *UEWiccan* journal, and is an example of a personalized rite.

Bonus Material-Ritual of the Compass Rose

Introduction

This ritual replaces the casting the circle or erecting the temple rite for European Diaspora[60] Wiccans who desire a non-Abrahamic but ceremonial magically valid all-purpose circle. This monograph presents a permanent protective version and a celebratory version appropriate for use with a ritual. It is not recommended for those unfamiliar with the four-point Wiccan circle used in British Traditional Wicca. It is also not recommended for non-Diaspora Wiccans.

The contemporary Wiccan circle is based on a Celtic cross, similar to that used in the woodcut "John Dee evoking a spirit" (left). In general form, it consists of two circles divided into quarters. The quarters may be literally drawn on the ground (as in the classical magical circle) or they may be represented by points at the edge of the circle. In this sense, it is more accurately described as a square or a cross within a circle.

For practical purposes, the square within the circle limits your working area and disrupts the energy flow in a space. Remember that energy in the form of wind, water, electricity or any other shape dislikes sharp angles and tends towards curves. More accurately, energy prefers to move in straight lines, but when encountering a sharp angle, tends to move in curves rather than sharp angles. Energy tends to bounce on hard angles, and the 90° angle is about as hard as

---

[60] The European Diaspora consists of people of traditionally European culture living outside of Europe.

you get. You need only blow on a mirror to experience what happens when air hits a perpendicular surface. Some of it is deflected back (in vortices) and some of it flattens and is dissipated into the natural air flow around the square.

It is for this reason that squares like that imagined in the above Dee woodcut are always softened, either appearing with an equilateral cross with an arm as a radius or appearing as a sort of squashed square, made up of semicircles. To maintain the separation of the angles and the outer circle, a larger circle is usually drawn outside the one touching the square of compass points. John Dee was well known to use the names of the angels on the inside and demons on the outside, and this (surprisingly) can be found on the woodcut itself.

The problem with the circle within the circle technique is that it reduces the functional limit of the energy of the inner and outer circles. Throw a third one in there, as Gardnerians often do, and you're talking about a waste of significant space, especially since he reduced the circle of the Key of Solomon from eighteen feet to nine. The Compass Rose solves this by using an octogram within a circle. Looking at the images below, you can see how the space within the octogram consists of obtuse angles, and the space without is a more organic space, more easily softened to a circle if desired. For practices in which it is necessary to deflect energy from outside the temple space, one need only leave the outer circle off altogether to create a highly refractive outer image. In fact, the octogram bounces energy from outside the shape and holds energy generated within or directed from above so well that its tendency to do this with light results in its being the most common gemstone cut.

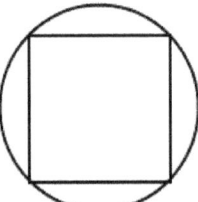 

It may be difficult at first to recognize the fact that the equilateral armed cross is a square, as we tend to think of squares as being perpendicular to our line of sight, and the equal armed Celtic cross (or solar cross) places the angles at a 45° angle to our bodies. If you take a piece of paper and just draw the points of the cross, you see at once that it is a square.

In addition to being less energetic than the octogram, the four point circle is less stable. Our religion agrees with Hermes Trismegistus that the large universe is a reflection of the small and vice versa. We can evaluate the stability of four-point systems and eight-point systems by evaluating their appearance in nature. A four-member ring is incredibly unstable. Cyclobutane, for example, has a boiling point of -91°C, making it darn near impossible to easily hold as a liquid by any typical means. Compare that with cyclooctane, which has a boiling point of 151°C and can even be a solid on a cold day. This energetic state exists in other materials, with eight-member rings common. Many flowers, for example, possess eight petals, or four petals and four sepals, and the evening primrose (the oil of which is used in this ritual) family, *left*, is composed of plants which have opposed petals and sepals in sets of four (forming an octogram) and petals in sets of eight[61].

Tufted evening-primrose, photo by Dave Powell of the USDA forest service; CCimage. The USDA/photographer of this picture makes no endorsement of this work or affiliated entities.

---

[61] Some domesticated evening primroses (genus *Oenathera*) have five petals, but most wild primroses do not. Most "five petaled primroses" are varieties of *Rosa Rugosa* (genus *Rosa*, not *Oenathera*).

The octogram has the added benefit of largely being unaffiliated with Abrahamic deities. The four-pointed temple is drenched in Abrahamic mythology, and this is why many inexperienced Wiccans tend to seek Abrahamic mythology when they feel the non-Abrahamic erecting the temple rites of their tradition are not good enough or are not valid for the purposes of Ceremonial Magic.

To understand this prejudice, you must first comprehend the Abrahamic mythology within the Key of Solomon. The Key of Solomon[62] is a 15th century collection of symbols of power and affiliated incantatio, generally in atrocious Hebrew. Most copies of it are based on an original or at least early Greek edition, including the seminal translation of Macgregor Mathers[63], which is assuredly the copy Gardner was following. Mathers did a wonderful job of restructuring the Hebrew, avoiding the mistakes of many other translators. The vast majority of modern translations, even those that claim to far exceed Mathers', are based upon his.

Based very loosely on what would become known as Kabala and falsely attributed to King Solomon, The Key of Solomon or *Clavis Salomonis* is often called a grimoire, but most grimoires of the time are *comprehensive*, discussing a system of magical techniques and giving the techniques and examples of what happens when the techniques are used. Since the Key of Solomon basically gives the preparations but not first person accounts of the results thereof, it is unlike the grimoires that inspired it, those that are contemporary with it, and those that followed it including the *Lemegeton*. Those books have the sort of recipe-book feel to them of most modern spellbooks. Grimoire, at its heart, means a book of the grammar of a system, and it is the grammar of Ceremonial Magic that The Key of Solomon lacks.

---

[62] Not to be confused with the (later) Lesser Key of Solomon.
[63] Mathers is generally believed to have relied heavily on the Colorno editions, but I've always been convinced he compiled his work from at least five editions, and this is only one of them.

The Key of Solomon is part of a vast system of Abrahamic Magic which is based upon some ideas that we find pretty abhorrent today...rightfully. In order to understand the ideas, however, you have to understand the fifteenth century Christian idea of what, exactly, made a person Jewish. Without going into detail, the general 15th century Christian, who'd probably never met a Jew, believed that Jews had secret knowledge of magic which they were not allowed to share outside their cabals. The very word cabal comes from Kabala, so if you can think of the sort of dark references the word cabal conjures up, you might get a clue about the view of Judaism in the minds of the creators of The Key.

Ceremonial Magic in this period of time was dominated by Christian mystics writing about secret Jewish doctrine that Jewish people, of course, had no knowledge of. Just like some modern Wiccans claim that they learned their craft from a now-deceased Great Grannie, so too do early authors and translators of grimoires claim that Great Grannie, or a cousin, or some other (deceased) relative was a Jew with access to that secret information. Most of this secret information was alleged to have been passed to the Jews directly from the Abrahamic deity. This information was either denied the Christians on purpose or by accident, depending on whose grimoires you read.

Unlike modern and primarily Protestant Christians, Christians in the fifteenth century didn't see magic as definitively evil and demonic. Even the use of demons wasn't considered dark or Satanic, but part of the Abrahamic deity's grand scheme of things. It was during the sixteenth century that the stigma of Abrahamic magic as dark and scary began to evolve, as Christianity evolved through wars and schisms into the multitraditional religion it is today.

Thomas Vaughan's *Magica Adamica* is an excellent introduction to the idea of magic as Christian entitlement. The idea, in short, is that the Abrahamic deity gave mankind magic as a parting gift as he was removed from paradise, a guaranteed way of surviving amongst the heathens and savages outside of Eden. You must understand that these very devout Christians were absolutely certain that magic was something that was of their god, biblically acceptable and a form of enacted communion with that god.

This magic was part of the ceremony of transubstantiation, and also found in alchemy, medicine, herbalism, astrology, astronomy and other "sciences" of the day. The Key of Solomon's science is primarily mathematics, with the pentacles (used here as geometric figures within a circle, not necessarily ones with five sides) largely representing geometry and astrology, and the intersection of the two.

Those who are particularly fond of the Key of Solomon will find that the primary astrological bodies represented by the octogram are Venus and Mars. While the Key of Solomon is based on Abrahamic mythology and The Ritual of the Compass Rose is not, the correspondences are still the same because astrology is loosely based on European indigenous gods. The Earth represents in many ways both the union and creation of Venus and Mars, and that should be kept in mind when conducting this ritual.

In the time since the creation of the mid-twentieth century magical circle, the depths of other Abrahamic mystics have been plumbed to add things to the circle. In the place of the classical elements and the four tools of magic represented in Tarot, people have chosen to add Paracelsus' elementals—Gnomes, Undines, Sylphs and Salamanders. These four things, in their core mythology, were granted dominion over the world by the Abrahamic god so that the world outside of Eden would be habitable for mankind. In Eden, these things were responsible for the work of keeping Eden's bounty. A good Christian, so the mages believed, could sway these servants of their god to his usage by performing secret tasks known about only by the Jews. The bounty of Eden, then, could be made on earth.

Again, the actual Jews knew nothing about this power they were alleged to have, which of course was regarded by the Christians as proof that they had it and were not sharing it with them…which would be comical if the Christians and their descendants did not use this as one of many despicable "justifications" for killing millions of Jews over hundreds of years. If you, as a Wiccan, have ever been accused of having a relationship with Satan by a right wing nutjob, you might have the slightest understanding of the feelings these Jews have experienced.

Moving past the love/hate relationship of Christian Magic and Judaism, one of the worst travesties of Ceremonial Magic in Wicca is the addition of the Watchtowers of John Dee (and Enochian Magic) to the erecting the temple rite. The audacity of such an act borders on Diabolism, but generally occurs out of pure ignorance. I think the Diabolism excuse would be better.

Dee and his lot flourished as England left Catholicism behind. It is not wholly inaccurate to say that these early Anglicans believed that the Vatican had magical resources equal to, or perhaps surpassing, the powers of the Jews. One of the remaining cultural beliefs of this group is that Latin somehow reverberates differently in the mind and therefore empowers magic differently, which is why many modern things employ Latin to sound more magical. Like Vaughan and the elementalists, Dee's magical system is rooted in the idea that humanity was kicked out of paradise for its wickedness and magic is one way their god, who is supposed to be omnibeneficient, seeks to make things right by his errant creations.

Dee and his contemporaries, like some of the Modern Christians who see Satan at every corner, thought that the top secret magic of the Jews that they received directly from their god was actually known to Christians, only now the people who were keeping it top secret were Catholics. The idea of top secret Catholic magic persists to this day, and it's a good hook to sell books with. The theory can be summed up this way: If an organization exists that any individual is not a member of (Masons, Pagans, Catholic Clergy, Jews, etc.) then the assumption is that the organization has top secret powers that warrant the exclusion of others. It's silly, really.

So Dee, fancying himself a scientist, "discovered" that by performing the right mathematical equations and revealing the complicated shapes of his own versions of the Solomanic "pentacles," he could cause the archangels to speak with the body of a channel, in his case Edward Kelley.[64] These "angels" spoke in a language which he called Enochian, and included a related symbology. The most important revelations of these angels are called The Enochian Calls.

It is without a doubt that at least some of the things the angels requested of Dee through Kelley were of Kelley's own making, including a wife-swapping episode, but believing the angels were real is a vital part of Enochiana, so I'll let that lie there where it may.

If you were not raised Christian, or you were raised in a tradition of Christianity that believed in a Sola Scriptura version of the mythos, you may have missed the Christian mythology that John Dee worked within, although it was common knowledge in his time, and fed numerous plays and poems, some of which, such as Dante's Inferno and Marlowe's Faustus, are still pretty good reading. Here, then, is a brief introduction to how the Christian world of John Dee worked:

> *In the beginning, there was a great big void. God was alone and decided that there should be more in the world, so he spoke all things into existence with the power of his words. He placed all things into a system where the sun and the moon and stars worked in a logical order. He was, in short, the architect of his universe.*
>
> *Eventually, God decided the universe needed population. He created the angels, and set them to keeping the world running. The angels did not have free will, so they obeyed him without thinking about it. The lack of ability to make decisions made these angels boring, so to serve as intermediaries be-*

---

[64] In some of his less lucid moments, Crowley claimed to be the reincarnation of Edward Kelley.

tween him and the angels, he created the archangels, who were stronger and smarter than the angels, and had free will.

There are hundreds of these archangels, but there are eight that are important to the Christian tradition, and those are Michael, Gabriel, Anael, Oriphiel, Raphael, Samael, Zachariel and, you guessed it, Lucifer.

Now, you have to bear in mind that Christian mystics literally spent days arguing over the nature of these angels. Some taught that Michael was not an angel at all, but an incarnation of God, a sort of mortal form he wore when he went to speak to mankind or do other tasks. In some of these traditions, Michael was actually the first thing God created, a sort of prototype of both mankind and Jesus. In the "let us make them in our image" debate, it is argued God is talking about himself and at least Michael when he uses the collective plural...but, anyways...

God created the world in layers. At the uppermost layer he abides in a physical form, and he collects all good things to him. In the lowest layer, the world farthest from him, lurks the stuff he dislikes and pushes away. He assigns his creation into these layers based on how well they turned out. One day, one of the archangels, Lucifer, gets sick of being a slave and takes over the lowest levels, deciding it's better to be a king of a terrible place than a slave in paradise. This only strengthens the gradient of the layers of the universe, making evil reside at the lowest levels, farthest from God, and God residing at the highest.

Eden is created fairly high up in the layered universe, and it is given its own equivalent of angels and archangels. Elementals are created to do the smallest tasks, and small animals, insects and the like are created to do their tasks as well. Unlike the elementals, angels and archangels, animals and insects are given the capacity to breed as they so wish. They are sent to fill the layers of the universe, with the ones with God's approval in the highest layers and the ones God hates the most at the lowest levels.

Mankind is created to fill Eden with life, and given the job to keep Eden under control and give order to the place. The first human gets a variety of mates before a female human is developed. He lives, happily, in his garden for hundreds of years, naming things, talking with the trees and animals (because everything in Eden is sentient) and living happily without clothes or shame in a world where food just grows on the branches and the water flows clear from the rock.

One day, one of the other sentient creatures in the garden, a dragon[65], one of the most beautiful of the creations, convinces the humans to eat the fruit of the only tree in the whole of the garden God said not to eat. This pisses God off, and the dragon and his descendants end up with no wings or feet or voices, doomed to crawl about on their belly. They are banished to the lowest levels of the universe, and made servants of Lucifer.

Humans are also punished, although less so. Women are given periods and painful childbirth and the protohumans are thrown down out of Eden and land in the central area of the layers of the universe, where they are still commanded to be fruitful and multiply, but now they are encountering the other humans cast out of Eden, animals that are dumb and violent and other things. Now, instead of keeping an ordered place in order, they must bring order to chaos.

Humans are still important, though. By making their new layer of the universe a reflection of heaven, they prevent the lower layers from growing. Unfortunately, since the

---

[65] It is often said this is Satan, but in traditional Christian mythology these are two different instances of bad guys.

laws of the universe are the same in all layers (as above, so below) it is always easier to descend into hell than it is to ascend into heaven, so mankind keeps giving in to temptation and failing.

First, God tries to help by giving people special powers, including talking with the animals and talking with the elementals and angels. When that fails, he leaves signs in the world about the order of things that skilled man can interpret. Still, mankind is evil, and is starting to not believe in God, so God takes a few of the descendants of the refugees from Eden, and many of the good animals, and puts them on a boat, and drowns most of the rest of the world. This gives his new people a chance to make a paradise out of the world, but soon they are returning to their old tricks.

When he destroyed the world, he promised he would not do it again, so now God limits himself to only destroying places where the evil is REALLY bad, and very concentrated. At first, he just uses his usual powers, earthquakes, lightning, raining brimstone, but this makes him really annoyed, and he gets sick of being the executioner, so he puts archangels and sky-riding powers called ἵππος, horses, to work.

The descendants of the original Eden refugees and the survivors of the Flood have a host of abilities at their hands to avoid being there when the powers ride through. They can talk to God, they have rituals and words that get his attention, and over time they've learned some of the words he used to speak the Universe into existence and a few other techniques to be safe, and they have a few near misses. God gives gifts to some of the people, like prophetic dreams, to help them out over time.

Since he doesn't want to spend his time looking at bad guys, he takes four of his best archangels and places them in towers at the four edges of the cen-

tral layer of the universe. From these towers, they keep an eye out for sin so he can surround himself only with the good things. He places the worst of all things, including his four horsemen, in the towers. Even the dragon that started the whole thing in Eden is chopped into four parts and one piece is placed in each tower. People are warned that they are being watched, but they still continue to stray.

In a last-ditch effort to save some of mankind from the impending opening of the towers, which will release the four horsemen and give the world over to evil, God inseminates a human female of the descendants of the Eden refugees and goes around in a human form telling them where they've strayed. He's especially concerned about the leaders of the remaining Edenites and their straying from the law.

Much blood has been spilled, and the old magic that God works with says that blood needs blood. To clean the slate, he sacrifices himself and this allows him to better understand the universe as mankind does. He is shown temptation, and he takes pity on mankind, giving them the chance to come and reside with him after their stint on earth is through, even if they were not perfect. The Guardians of the Watchtowers are quelled, and they are told to keep looking, but to keep the reigns tight on the horsemen and the other criminals and bad things that live in the towers. His stint as a human has packed these towers with the wicked who are too wicked to trust to hell, because they might escape…A couple of Herods, an Apostle and half of the elders of the province of Judea are added to the towers in this time period.

The creation of such good in the universe as his own son/avatar meant that evil had to be added to the universe in the same amount, or the material plane of earth would be demolished by shifting in *its place in the layers. God must fight a constant battle to keep things where they belong, because that's how the system he made operates, and he likes it that way, but it still has rules. This new evil demigod, an anti-Christ, is kept in the towers.*

The archangels, though, are creatures of total free will, and while God is forgiving, they are not, and if the world gets evil enough, they will open the gates and let out the four horsemen, the antichrist, the powers of fire, water, earth and air and a host of baddies that live in the towers. Before that happens, God will give a bunch of signs to his chosen people, who may be spared.

Once the evil has had its way with the material plane, it will turn on itself and a new era of goodness and a new Eden will be created. All good things will be housed in the new Eden and the cycle will start again.

There are a number of things you must get from this story to understand the mechanism of the magic circle of Dee. First, you must understand that calling the elementals is nonsense even to ceremonial mages. Command of the elementals shows that you have power over an element, and does not have anything to do with the circle but is proof of one's connection to the creator of Eden. It is evidence of one's godliness. Remember, also, that the authors of Christian elemental magic believed that these elementals were absolutely detectable if you could see heat or cold or travel deep in the earth. These were things they expected scientific proof of.

Calling the Guardians of the Watchtowers or the archangels in the magic circle was designed to lend power to your rite by virtue of the eyes of the Guardians. A shade or dead spirit would be compelled to be absolutely truthful because an untruth before the Guardians could result in a one-way trip into the prisons of the towers. You got the guardian's attention by use of their names, which were full of power because they were the names God used to speak them into existence. The Hebrew (and later the Latin) names of these beings and things associated with God were considered to have innate power. Consider the invocation of the Lesser Banishing Ritual of the Pentagram as another example.

The Ceremonial Magic circle which is cropped for use in Wicca is a Christian-based creation which uses the powers of the Christian god and the Will of the Wiccan to hold the power and direct it as needed. This Compass Rose temple Rite is not centered upon the Christian God, but centered upon the Will and Self of the Wiccan using it. It invokes the ancestors of the Wiccan and his ancestral gods and the power of the Wiccan himself, and does not require the use of foreign gods.

Wicca is an inherently polytheistic European system. When the magic circle is cast within Europe, it should involve summoning or invoking the genus loci of a place at a place of power of said genus loci or dedicating the space to the local gods. An octogram works perfectly for this as well, and you can see this at such places as Stonehenge, where a reflection of the central stones though the center of the their outer pairs, left makes a perfect octogram, albeit offset from the center of the circle itself. (in the diagram, black represents stone pairs existing at one time and gray represents the stones needed to complete the octogram.

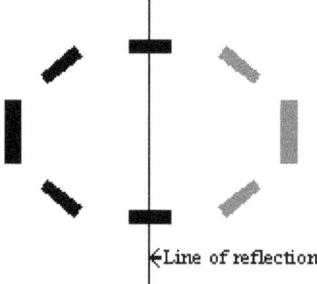

The most powerful octogram is actually not the perfect square I use for the Compass Rose symbol, but the double-pentagram octogram, which some might recognize from elsewhere in ceremonial magic. It is very easy, however, to trace this into your permanent octogram for the temple Rite and make a very strong geometric symbol. I've squashed this one a little to bring out the pentagrams:

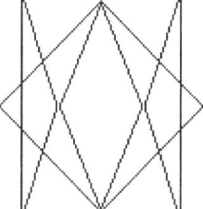

It can be hard to see, but this symbol incorporates the hexagram, pentagram and a number of other potent signs, especially when the bisectors are added, not just visualized. In the second one, I've highlighted a pentagram.

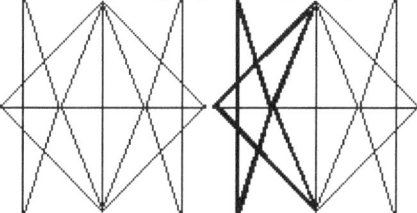

The idea that five plus five yields eight is potent in ceremonial magic, because it defies logic, but is still logical. It is impossible to make two pentagrams touch at more than two points, and the shape it makes when it does is fascinating because that shape is also two squares. For someone like John Dee, this shape would've been mind bogglingly complex.

That being said, it does take more than a little bit of guts to take something as standard as the four point Wiccan magical circle and abandon it for something like this, even if this is inherently better. Since our octogram is based on the simple forty-five degree rotation of one square upon the other, it lends itself to casting a contemporary circle upon it when it is built, so there is no need to remove the more potent temple for the casting of a simple celebratory rite.

Erecting the Permanent Temple

The traditional Wiccan temple rite is non-fixed, we are told, because the original Witches the religion is based upon had to make all of their ritual gear from household implements and the gear required a sort of plausible deniability to throw off the hounds of the magistrates. "Why constable," we imagine these ancestors saying, "That's the caldron I do my laundry in, and the knives are for cutting rutabagas!"

The problem, of course, is that there is only an imagined relationship between Wiccans and these ancient cunning-folk, and avoiding permanent temple structures in homage to them is a mistake. If you have the space, it is perfectly acceptable to do as the mages do and create a permanent conjury.[66] This technique for erecting the physical spaces of the conjury can be scaled down to the top of the table if so desired, and pressed out into any space using the Principle of Sympathy. It is presented here in the fullest form with the knowledge that most will have to scale it down as appropriate. A celebratory rite calling up the circle without constructing the physical conjury is presented later in this work. Familiarity with the techniques of setting up the physical conjury is beneficial to the technique of setting up a temporary circle, so this section is still worthwhile for those of you who cannot afford the time, energy and supplies of the conjury.

Begin by using a floating compass (also called a needle or analog compass) to find the magnetic north of your desired location. You will be designing the space to change as magnetic north changes. This makes north, not east, the anchor of the circle. You must verify that magnetic north is still at the north mark of your circle before each circle. The hardest change between the Compass Rose rite of erecting the temple and the four-point circle is the change from east as an anchor to north. Note, of course, that if you are in the Southern Hemisphere, you may need to use magnetic south

---

[66] Pronounced, in this usage, as con-your-ee.

to calculate magnetic north. You can use a simple 180° rotation for all intents and purposes.

Since the Compass Rose rite is designed to work with energy flows, not truly the map points, you don't need to correct your location to true bearing. Don't worry about the declination angle, because for this rite your compass' north is north. In the event of a massive magnetic shift, in which the South Pole becomes stronger than the North Pole, you can base your magnetic north on the 180° rotation of the South Pole, but the position of the winds should remain, as the wind names and properties are based on what the winds have done, historically, in Europe, not based on what the winds may be doing now.

You should realign your circle with magnetic north, or at least verify the alignment, once a year.

One you have established magnetic north, draw a line from north to south that is three meters long. You've now drawn the radius of the conjury's circle. Place a stake or sword at the end of this line, in what will become the heart of the temple. This sword must have a cylindrical hilt. Take a six meter long cord and pass it through an iron ring that will fit over the sword. Doubling it precisely, make a larkshead[67] over the ring and pass the ring over the hilt of the sword. Holding the ends in your hand, stand at your Magnetic North and hold the cord taut.

Walk from the north to the south, clockwise, and back to the north, tracing the path of the circle and marking as you go, until you've traced out a perfect circle. Check your north again. If you absolutely cannot ever change the orientation of your temple (for example, you're building a room around it and want the door at north) you can build a false

---

[67] Fold cord in half. Pass the rounded part of the fold through the ring. Pass the ends of the cord through the loop and pull tight, thuswise:

magnetic north by placing a large rare earth magnet at the north end of your circle, and sinking it beneath the floor.[68]

Once you've traced your circle, (and sunk your magnet, if you feel so inclined,) you're ready to prepare the floor. If you're doing it outside, I recommend using concrete in which you've replaced 1/10 of your aggregate with ferrous ore or iron filings, being aware that they *will* rust if exposed to rain and your concrete will be stained. For the rest of us, I'm assuming your temple is protected from the elements, at least partially, and from now on I will speak exclusively thereof.

Scrub the floor where the circle is to be formed with a 2:1 blend of appropriate holy or blessed water and Atlantic Ocean sea water. If available, soak a linen or cotton bag of dried hyssop in the water before using. Scrub in circular, clockwise motions from within the circle to without. Use cotton, linen or natural sponge, do not use plastic or metal.

Allow to dry overnight. Then paint the interior of the circle, from North to South, with a magnetic primer, or a conventional primer to which a substantial amount of magnetic paint additive has been added. Magnetic paint additive is not magnetic itself but contains minute iron particles to which a magnet will stick. These particles will align with the earth's magnetic field as well as provide the usual benefits of iron in the circle. You are, in essence, creating a space that is dead to the energy beneath you. Paint a minimum of four coats of the stuff.

Once you have a fully dry, fully primed surface, combine 3 drops each of Rose Otto and Labdanum oil into 0.5mL of evening primrose oil. Add this to 1L of olive oil. Take the resulting mixture and scrub the painted area. Allow to sit for one day, then buff with paper towels or cotton cloth until there is no sign of shininess on the towels. Over this, paint four more coats of the magnetic paint. Allow to dry thoroughly.

---

[68] If, for some bizarre reason, you use an enormous one, make sure to leave appropriate signage around warning people.

It is possible to do this treatment to an entire floor of a room, as in a basement, and then draw the circle atop it.

Place a top coat of paint on this one to protect it. If you use a chalkboard additive you can draw the circle on the floor with chalk, which is very nifty. You can also use standard floor paint, but since you should be barefoot in the circle, all but the most delicate of paints will hold up. Allow the paint to dry and cure as per manufacturer's directions.

Using paint (preferably copper or gold in color) paint a circle on the outer edge of the temple boundary. This is the line you will not be crossing during your temple rite. Ideally, each of the painting coats and lines drawn are enhanced energetically, but it is possible for someone with no skill at manipulating energy to create such a thing as well. It is possible to purchase paint made of genuine copper, and if you can do this, that's wonderful, as it makes the traditional channel filled with copper solder a lot easier to use. Remember that traditionally, iron blocks energy and steel, copper and silver move it around and provide a place where it tends to pool. Within this circle, approximately the length of your hand apart, place another circle.

Mark the north, east, south and west points on this inner circle. Then mark the cross points. Draw a line from north to east, east to south, south to west, etc. Draw another line from northwest to southwest, etc. Now, walking around the circle to find the exact point where a central circle touches no line, trace a third inner line. Your space should now resemble this:

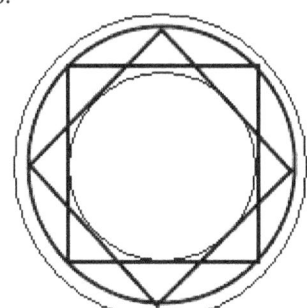

Using paint, or chalk, color the traditional cardinal points black (or gray, if your floor is black.)

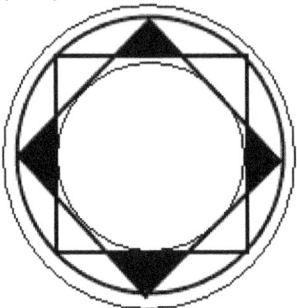

Then, using blue, paint the remaining points.

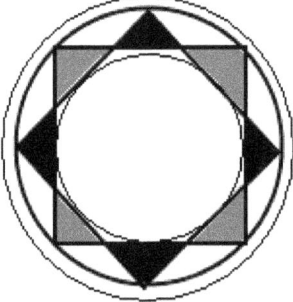

Paint the exterior triangles red.

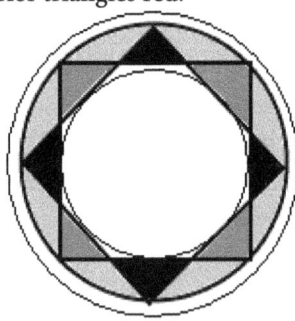

These colors represent the three ink colors of classical mapmakers. They also, with white, represent the four characteristics of humanity. White for purity and sacrifice (think bone, which is classically burned on pyres as an offering to the gods,) red for passion and blood, blue for restraint and strength and black for the ability to build and use technology. This is a gross oversimplification, but it's less oversimplified than the idea that they represent "spirit, mind, body and intellect."

At the points of the compass, write the names of the eight winds. If it makes you feel better to write them in Theban, then do so. The script should be within the outer circle, between the outer barrier and the circle touching the points. You can also just write the first syllable of the winds, as those will be used in the incantation. If you are unfamiliar with the names of the winds, as you go clockwise in the circle, they are: Tramontana, Greco, Levante, Siroco, Ostro, Libeccio, Ponente and Maestro.

Burn asafetida or an excess of labdanum[69] to clear the space of any energies, and bless the temple once the smell has cleared.

---

[69] Sagebrush is probably an effective alternate.

Erecting the Temporary Temple

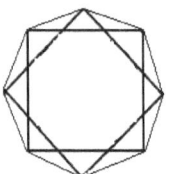
If outside, use stakes and ropes to mark out the eight points and their lines, or pour a rough estimate of the shapes out with something harmless, like flour or sawdust. Clearly mark the points of the winds. If indoors, use tape. It is permissible in this case to make your outer circle into an octagon, left.

Place a glass containing water at each point and float a floating candle within it. By doing this, you cancel out the effect of the fire at each point, rendering the elements at each point inherently stable. Remember that the compass rose does not associate the elements with directions, as the traditional circle does, but instead invokes all elements as being of one place.

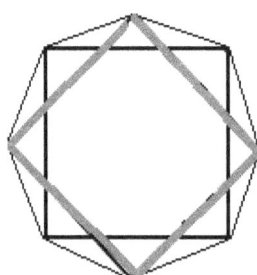
Visualize a line of blackness as you walk clockwise from the north along the diamond path. See it shielding the space within. I have highlighted the diamond path in gray to the left. The diamond path represents those actions that are selfless, doing primarily for others, but do not confuse it with actions that are purely good. When you have finished, stand facing each of the compass points and intone the first syllable of each of the four cardinal winds.

Step to the northwest, and walk the square path (the other square in the octogram) counterclockwise. This should be visualized as blue. The square path represents those actions that are selfish, doing primarily for yourself. Do not confuse this with evil, however. When you have finished, stand facing each of the cross compass points and intone the first syllable of the remaining winds.

Step to the north and walk the outer path, visualizing red light. This is the path of the outside, of relationships with other people and physical entities. The outer path is the path of strength that comes from outside one's self and should not be seen as anything else. When you reach the center, announce who you are and what you are doing there. The blessing of the space should follow shortly. Feel free to announce this to your participants at this time.

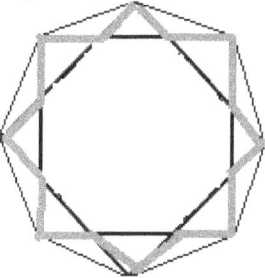

The Outer Path

Next, walk the inner path, the octagon at the heart of the octogram, visualizing white light. This is the path of the self, and represents the relationships to your gods and your ancestors. When finished, stand at the center and say an appropriate prayer or intonation, obviously, you have to find this within.

Commence with the blessing of the temple and the calling of the winds.

Note that this also works well for energetically enhancing the permanent space.

Blessing the temple (Calling the winds)

Have all participants stand in the eye (the central circle) of the octogram. Stand at the north, and slowly intone the name of the wind. Tramontana. Turn 180° and face your participants, if any. To them, or to the wind, say "Across the mountains, from the skies, the north wind, bitter, violent flies. Bringing snow and bringing rain, she also brings the end of pain, for when a person starts to roam, it is from north he finds his home.[70]"

Intone again the name of the wind, holding it until you feel or hear the wind's response. When that occurs, light a floating candle submerged in a glass of water to mark your acknowledgement of the wind. Use a long wooden match, and quench the match in the water before moving onward. At each point you will neutralize earth, air, fire and water in this fashion, leaving only the energy of the winds.

Walk the complete path to the northeast. The first six parts of the complete path are shown below. The path represents the whole of the universe and also the diaspora itself, wandering around the universe while always remaining connected to the clan, the family and land that they sprung from, and the associated gods. I will not illustrate the whole path, but you can replicate it easily from 6 onward. Just walk the entire symbol without taking the same path. You can start at true north, but I prefer this starting location.

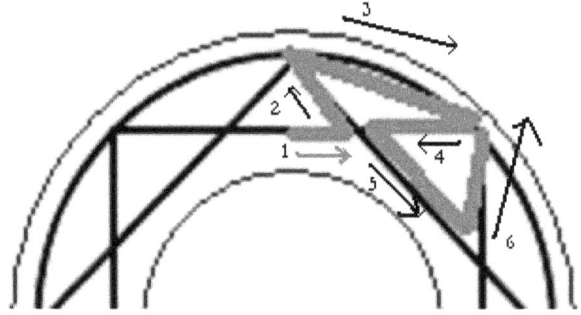

[70] It is not necessary to do this in verse. The real guts of the rite are the unspoken words. The verse here is presented in translation of my own version of this rite and is thus imperfect. I also find merely greeting the winds works as well.

When you get to the northeast, repeat the steps with Greco, instead. Remember it is Greh-co, not gree-co. "From Pelion's sacred slopes, the northeast blows, bringing the warmth of the east but also northern snows. It brings the smell of rich warm earth, but pushes you from it with mirth."

At Levante: "Rising from the sun's birth to warm the west and heat the earth, the east wind faces many foes but always overpowers those, passing or' the strongest lees, through the Pillars of Heracles."

At Siroco: "Often colored with gold or rust, the southeast wind fills the sky with dust. Before the death bell's bitter knell, if you seek her paradise you'll find her hell."

At Ostro: "Pregnant with heat and rain, the south-wind brings both death and life, her seething vapor, water laden breeds both plenty and strife. When from the south the wind does blow, rain and heat or heavy snow."

At Libeccio: "Changeable southwest, sometimes steady as a wall, calm and bright until she explodes in a squall. Seek in her the bountiful islands or arid coast, or stormy highlands, where she changes the most."

At Ponente: "West wind, blowing from where it ends to where it begins, making kings of paupers — subtlest of winds. Your silent force is rarely felt although with your results we've often dealt."

At Maestro: "Northwest, wind most blessed, bringing the strength of the north and the change of the west. Stabilizing, warming, most favored as you roam, gentlest wind that brings me home."

Back to the North: "Now are the eight winds called to this rite, heed my call this sacred night."

Erecting the Tower of the Winds.

The Tower of the Winds is the power structure you are going to erect in which to hold the energies generated by the rite. You should visualize an octagonal structure tapering above your head, with each of the winds in balance, pushing towards the center and being forced up and out. As you build energy in your accustomed manner, it will fill to the point of breaking. When it is time to break it, call the wind(s) that will carry the energy to its destination and break the circle at that point by spilling the water and extinguishing the candle...cutting the cord or smearing the chalk if a temporary circle.

Note that while it is polite to thank the winds, it is not required to destroy the temple once you have erected it, you can leave the energy structure's remains for the next time you build the temple. The act of releasing the power alone breaks the temple.

Into a libation dish, or onto the ground, pour a sacrifice of wine and grain to each of the winds, speaking their names from north to northwest (Boreas, Kaikias, Euros, Apeliotes, Notus, Livos, Zephyrus, and Skiron.) Burn appropriate sacrifices (such as laurel or sage) to other deities involved in the rite.

Fill the tower clockwise, beginning at the bottom, as you would with a contemporary cone of power. The rest is straightforward energy manipulation, really quite simple.

Some Notes:

It's possible to do the rite small scale by sketching the symbols on a table top and using the principle of sympathy and your own personal energy to move the functional lines out. I've also done this using a round altar instead of moving around a circle with people standing in it. It will require a bit more skill, but it's a very functional workaround.

As an erecting the temple rite, this is not a ritual in and of itself, but is, instead, a place to do a rite. It's not uncommon for the Wiccan circle to throw some stuff from the actual ritual into the circle casting, and this ritual assumes you have the know-how to move stuff in and out of the casting as desired. The only thing this replaces is the bastardized Solomanic circle Gardner invented.

It's important to recognize this is not a UEW rite, it's a MacMorgan Covenstead one, and while it's being distributed free to UEWwies I personally trust, it's pretty much going to be worthless to people lacking a certain set of skills and vocabulary. To prevent it from being passed around like a batch of chocolate brownies in a dorm room, I've made a download and print version of this available for a fee. If you use this rite in a public forum, I ask that you tell people where it came from and allow them to purchase their own copies.

Insert your own disclaimers here.

Kat.

Bonus Material-The Elemental Visualizations

Reprinted from *All One Wicca*, used with permission.

In Universal Eclectic Wicca, the elements also represent states to achieve and in larger circles and some private ones, the elements are invoked as examples of our inner power, "that we may be like" that element. Visualization[71] is often used to initiate the Wiccan to the path of that element, and the inner powers or states discovered are used in Ritual and everyday life.

These visualizations include each element, with a focus on the power of one and the state to be achieved. In group situations, these visualizations are read by one person, often with drumming or instrumental music in the background, at home, a tape player should be used to record the words of the visualization until you no longer need them. Wear comfortable clothes, even use a blanket if you wish, and lie on your back with your hands on your stomach. Breathe in slowly, then hold the breath for three seconds, then slowly exhale. You should feel your stomach rise with each breath, if not, put a book or some small weight on your stomach and practice making it move up and down slightly with your breathing.

Don't worry about doing the visualizations **now**, just slow down, be still, and wait for it to come. You may wish to practice these breathing techniques without visualization for a short time each night until they become comfortable—if you fall asleep at any point, don't fret, it just means you reached a **very** intense point of relaxation, and you probably needed the sleep more than you needed the visualization.

Distraction during visualization should be avoided, and this includes "Ohmigods I gotta go to work in two hours," so practice visualization with a loose schedule, and turn off the television and the radio. After a while, the states you may achieve through visualization may become instant, and then distraction doesn't matter. Feel

---

[71] A certain fundamentalist Christian author describes visualization as indoctrination and "cult mind-control," and while nearly everyone knows that's a load of bull, by all means stop doing it if you are being mind-controlled by a cult or indoctrinated into something!

free to change any aspects you feel uncomfortable with in the visualization. If sitting in a chair or a Yoga stance works better for you, that is how you should perform the visualization. These are all suggestions, none of this is written in stone.

Grounding: The Earth Visualization

Lie flat on your back in a field, if you do not have access to a field, lie on a floor and first visualize through the steel, wood and concrete. Feel yourself falling until you are lying in the dust below your foundation, and "Touch" the permeable earth that's there…

Reach through the earth into the tiny wormholes permeating the soil. Feel each nerve on your finger extend forward like a root hair system. You cannot move your fingers.

The creatures of the soil, things you once feared perhaps, pass over you, the strands of your hair. Your hair grows impossibly fast, rooting itself to the ground, entangling itself with your fingers. You cannot move your head…

An energy tingles in your chest, and all the stresses and anxieties grow out as roots through your body and hairs, strengthening you, reaching miles and miles down to an underground lake. You feel from above as each root plunges into the earth warmed water, and as the very last root plunges in, you feel a bitter cold taking over the rest of you, trying to suck every inch of warmth from your bones. You feel the cold sucked through the rest of your body toward the roots, heat slowly returning to your face. You see the cold sucked into the water, forming a silverish slick that bubbles slowly as the pure water milks it from your roots.

A wind springs up in the underground cavern, twisting the ends of your roots and tossing the silver about frantically, painting the walls with it and throwing your roots around viciously. Only the knurled roots of your worries are affected, twisting, bending, but never breaking, still holding you as firm as you need.

Without warning, the wind subsides. The silver light covers everything except the water, which is clear once more. The rocks, your roots, even the walls of the cavern all glow with the light.

The warmth of the lake pushes into you, replacing what the storm drained. You feel the pulse of the water, though you …though the earth…the beat rushes through every inch of you, and you begin to notice the light moving with the pulse, slowly creeping toward you. A closer look shows the silver light to be thousands of bioluminescent creatures, no larger than fleas and they swarm silently to you, covering you in a living, pulsing shield.

A column of steam rises from the water, and you feel the heat blocked by the creatures. They melt into every inch of you as the steam and water buffet you, keeping you from burning and tempering you into a solid coat of light. Your senses thus transmuted, the steam stops, and your roots slowly retract, bringing the light into your body...you feel it just beneath the skin, a tingle of deeper strength. As you open your eyes, you know it's there ...you are aware of the difference, and this feeling, this memory is forever. You are changed ...you are grounded.

Many (but not all) people experience grounding the first time they practice this visualization. It is not actually a metamorphosis, but a way of rerouting power into a force you already possess. For some, merely lying in bed, or any other personal place, is a way to achieve this state ...experiment. When you achieve that anchored feeling, try to remember the sensation in detail. Practice will make it come easier.

The Womb: The Water Visualization

For this exercise, you want to lie on your back, with your arms crossed over your chest. The healing state we're attempting to achieve here is the "mentally pure" state that some rituals, especially those involved with healing, call for. If you have already achieved a grounded state, try grounding yourself before attempting the visualization. Transference from one state to the next is easier than transference from everyday action to metaphysical action. I've listed the states in order of easiest to hardest for this purpose.

(If you have a tape of ocean waves, play it now, if you have an ocean drum, try sitting in a comfortable chair with the drum on your lap and slowly rock in a circular motion, if you have no way to hear waves, you'll just have to listen to your heartbeat and imagine the rushing in and out of sound.)

Breathe in, and let that breath be the slow roll of the waves coming in to shore, breathe out and feel it roll away. Let this continue, the rolling in and out, until you begin to feel a lightness around your body ...imagine the soft feel of warm water as it laps at your toes, your feet, your ankles, lifting them from the ground and gently pulling you into the water. Your legs, your hips, your back, touch the water as you float up, carried on the water effortlessly, and at once, you're floating, carried by the warm water with no fear of sinking.

The waves increase in speed, pulling you further from land with each new downbeat, and you begin to feel the sun beating upon you, trying to sink you beneath the waves with a heat you feel like a physical pressure. The water beneath you rumbles in fierce protectiveness, and you are rushed upward toward a deep blue sky. Impossibly light, you are tossed off of the cresting waves and into the sky, where you gently lift into an updraft, then spiral down onto a outstretched arm of water, which caresses your body as you land, pulling you down beneath the waves. Your first breath as you sink is difficult, but your body readjusts to the act of water breathing, remembering pre-infancy instinct. The warmth fills you, inside and out, as you are tossed gently, current to current. The water gently flows through your hair, pulling away the dirt of the common world and leaving you pure and innocent. You see yourself rushing toward the skin of the water, the sunlight playing on it like a fragmented mirror that seems more and more solid as you flow closer. You hit the barrier, and feel it refuse to yield. The pressure builds up behind you, pushing harder, and you are thrust out, taking your first breath of air violently and loud, the pressure exploding from your body. Pulled on by a million gentle fingers, you are carried to the shore, where the earth grows solid beneath your feet. You are truly reborn.

As with the other visualizations, this is only a suggestion, a technique that may or may not help you experience this sensation. Again, we deal here with the difficulty of our languages, for these states, being personal and varied, are indescribable as well.

Astral Consciousness: The Air Visualization

Air is not only an element of purification, but is also the element of the free mind. For that reason, students of astral projection often use visualizations as launching boards into their astral travels. I make no claims about the validity of astral travel, because there is no strict definition of it, and no grounded scientific proof. In no way am I saying it does *not* exist either, discussion of such levels of metaphysics are best left to metaphysical tomes, not books on Wicca. Let me reiterate here, that magic, metaphysics and New Age practices are something many Wiccans do, but are not part of the actual religion. Ritual magic, which is really advanced prayer, will be covered in a later chapter.

Self-hypnosis is recommended for this visualization, or a period of meditation preceding it. If you find that the imagery makes you uncomfortable, but not enough to want to not do it, you may wish to cast a circle (next chapter) or wear a protective piece of jewelry. Another idea, carry a small stone in your hand, to remind you of earth. The deep breathing you do here should be enough to keep you from feeling weird, but if you feel that you are out-of-body prone, do what you need to do to ground yourself or give yourself protection from a possible negative experience. If you have enough metaphysical background to enter reverie while performing this visualization, all the better for you.

Begin with the breathing you've used in other exercises, but with each exhale, feel your extremities slowly begin to go numb...first your fingers and toes, then your hands and feet, all the way up to your neck...try not to move these numb parts, but let twitches, and other unconscious movements happen. When only your head seems moveable, visualize a network of threads of light holding you down. You can feel these threads holding down your power, but as you assert yourself, the tiny threads begin to snap, your body slowly rising as each thread ceases to hold you down. You float carelessly through the air, turning to see your motionless body lying on the floor behind you. You smile, and a few seconds pass before the smile reaches your face below you. You notice a silver umbilical cord tying you to your body, which is safe on the guardian earth, without a further care, you turn and drift up, through the rafters, the roof, whatever, into the night sky. You push yourself up, (optional: past the lights of the city, the smog and heat until you come to pure air) into a black sky dotted with millions of stars. A wind, carrying an electric charge so fierce that you can smell it, pushes you around until you are inches away from a wall of glowing light, which shimmers with pulses of color like minute lightning flashes. You reach out and touch the wall, and are sucked into a fast moving stream of light and air, which carries you impossibly fast. From your position within the wall, you can see the semi-sphere of a far-off earth, blue-green and brown behind you. the lights of cities twinkle like Christmas lights, adding to its splendor, and a network of paths similar to the one you are on encircle it in a warm net. You step out of the wall into another and are pulled in another direction, toward black clouds which butt up against each other in angry protest. You enter these clouds, dropping out of the energy stream, and feel the caress of lightning as it passes through you. A weight begins to fill you, and you drop several inches, the pressure strong enough to make you feel as if you're about to explode. With a great rip of thunder, the rain begins and the pressure begins to ease, the water pouring through the clouds and through you onto the ground below. Rained out, you feel a little drained, so you hook the energy stream once more, feeling its energy revitalize you. You float some more, allowing yourself to be tossed about by the wind and the energy fields, until you see a circle of stones beneath you, like Stonehenge, only smaller. You touch upon the stone at the center of the ring and feel an energy from it, similar to the one in the wall. You allow yourself to join with the stone's energy for a moment, then press off once more, finding an equilibrium between the draw of the earthy stone and the airy fields of energy. You point a finger at the stone, and a line of energy crackles from your hand and reaches it. You can see energy from the stone trickling into the line, and feel it filling your hand, with your other hand, you create a line between your body and the energy field above you, and for a few moments, you are pulled by the two forces, which yield to you and begin to strengthen you. After a few moments, you allow the lines to disintegrate, knowing you can draw in no more power. You place your hands palm to palm and a globe of energy forms around you. You concentrate for a moment, noticing the umbilical that stretches the miles to your body. You watch as it detaches from you and attaches to the bubble. There is a sucking sound, and your ears pop, and you find yourself standing above your body. You stretch out your hands, and the bubble melds into the body as energy crackles from your hands and is pulled into the body. You allow your left hand to drain itself dry, and then watch as your right hand begins to disintegrate, fingers, arms, shoulder, all forming into lines of light, you look briefly before you allow yourself to be fully drawn back, and notice the smile is still there, peaceful, and serene...you notice as you regain control of your limbs that the little threads do not reform, you've escaped them, and if they come back, it will be at your request.

This is only a test…The Fire Visualization

The Fire Visualization creates the mindset of a challenger, a very powerful thinking and feeling method, which we train ourselves in. The Fire consciousness is usefully invoked at any time where we must be grounded through pain, or even in so called lesser stresses like exams, or defending a thesis. There is a feeling of being drawn or directed in this visualization, like the soul has more important things to do than the body does. This can help put you into perspective about your life. Are your greatest worries really as bad as all that?

Begin this visualization like the others; only make sure you're warm when you do it. A friend of mine suggests using the visualization while tanning, but I love my skin too much to try[72]. This visualization is best done during the day, although a more imaginative person might imagine traveling around the world before rising into the sun. If at anytime you are uncomfortable, change the visualization. Remember; never do anything you don't want to do!

You feel your body dissolving, breaking down into spherical molecules of black carbon. You are, all at once, more aware of your being than ever. Your heart still beats, your lungs still breathe, but you are made of millions of seething particles. Breathe deep and let the particles float like a flock of swallows into the sky. You curve, you undulate, but all the while you are one, held together by the invisible threads of molecular bonding, you are a great cloud of smoke across the sky, turning the sun blood red as it passes through you. You stand, at once, both under and above yourself. You touch the molecules of smoke and they cling to your mind's fingers, lifting you up, up into the blood red sunlight. Your mind's eyes close for a moment and they are the red of your eyelids, when you open them again you see only the sunlight, impossibly close and impossibly red. The sunlight illuminates your particles as they lift your mind's body toward the red sun, an impossible carpet of red and gold that warms as you approach the sphere. You feel your blood pounding and no-

---

[72] As a person who has worked in research for a Cancer center, let me reiterate…don't tan. Tanning and smoking… don't do them!

tice it's the pounding of the sun. In, hold, out, you breathe, red, gold, orange, it flashes. The beat grows louder. Red. Orange. Gold. You stretch your fingers toward the sun and they are tinged with the clear white of diamonds and quartz, the color drained away into the pounding sun. Your body tingles with the heat, like a hot shower after a cool swim, and you breathe through it, in, out, in, until the heat becomes soothing instead of harsh. The colors change, Red. Orange. Gold. Violet. White. Blue. The heat is so intense it actually cools you. This is the heat of wintergreen, of menthol, and the dust of your magic carpet is the crystal blue-white of ash so pure it resembles snow. A yellow haze forms between you and the sun, so large now that you can see nothing else. The yellow haze comes closer and you see that it is a wall of pale fire, its color the color of fresh lemons, tinged on the outer edge with the blue-white of the hottest flames. With a whoosh you pass through it, and it clings to you like some kind of membrane. The sun is now the deep red color of burning coals and you turn, feet towards the sun and gently float to the surface, held aloft for ages by the heat while pulled forward by the inescapable gravity. Your feet touch the spongy surface of the sun, and you feel no more than the deep heat of your blood. The pounding turns metallic, and you walk towards it. A being of pure fire appears before you, hammering a crystal blade at a forge. He points behind you and you see your footprints lingering on the sun, a patch of black-red coals that ignite slowly into the red of the flaming ground beneath you. You turn back to him and he holds the sword out to you, hilt first. You take it, and he turns into a giant lizard of flame, the great salamander. He roars at you, and you recognize it as a challenge. The sword pulses in your hand as the salamander swipes at you. You dodge and he swishes his lizard tail at you, you dodge once more and swing the sword in a wild arc at the creature. In the moment of connection, the salamander's lizard-like face is aglow with pride in you, his student. His head connects with the blade and disappears in a puff of white smoke. The body fizzles away in a cloud of steam and you find yourself walking through dense orange-tinged fog. The ruins of a great marble temple are before you, and you step up upon a marble dais, soft and cold beneath your ash covered feet. A woman, clad in a white gown nods at you and holds her hand out. You give her the sword and she ges-

tures for you to reach into a small well and remove the huge gem that lies within it. As you lift the gem a jet of white flame pushes you up, up into the sky and away from the surface of the sun. The gem pulls you into blackness, and then, slowly, you approach the earth. The blackness turns to blue as the gem points your feet towards home. It quivers in your grip and pulls away from you, and you find yourself plummeting back toward the earth and slamming into your body as the gem climbs deeper into space.. Before you can breathe another breath, you see the gem, through the roof, through the sky, as it explodes in white hot fire and a star appears in the heavens. Your star.

This visualization is optional, more so than the others. In a Universal Eclectic Wicca circle, instead of using visualization to "discover" the fire consciousness, we usually suggest a "test" of some kind, a fear one might need to conquer. A "trial by Fire" often has very little to do with the actual element, and more to deal with what is called its Sphere of Influence. The Sphere of Influence of an element includes the spiritual and mythological meanings a person or culture attributes to it.

Bonus Material-The Heraldic Circle

Part One: From UEWiccan, May 2007

I am terribly uncomfortable casting a circle for a large group, as most of those who have had a ritual with me have found. Our dear Jenny and Phoenix have both been put on the spot as I shirked my duty to the gathering. My biggest excuse is that I am simply not comfortable in a situation meeting others expectations of what a good circle should be, but the easiest way to get out of it is remind people that you're the teacher and you need to see them do it…

…It is with the caveat of that discomfort and shirkism that I ask for understanding in this discussion of one way I change my personal circles from the UEW norm. In my case, this adaptation is so strong and personal for me that I just don't do group circles anymore because they don't feel as tight on a metaphysical level as my personal ones do. I present my example not so that you can do the same, as it would be meaningless to you, but to lead others to share how they adapt simple rituals to their personal practice to find deeper relevance in the simplest act.

The compass points of the Wiccan circle stand complete as originally written into the liturgy, without the addition of the elementals of Paracelsus or the archangels of John Dee. Wiccans with too much time on their hands and too little knowledge of Ceremonial Magic(k) have been adding to the circle during the whole of Wicca's brief existence, which (perhaps surprisingly) tends to not make the circle rite stronger, but weaker. They are adding because they think the circle *must be more* than the rite it is, and this is not the same as adding to make the circle *your own*.

The idea of the Wiccan circle is a space beyond space and a time beyond time. We don't cast the circle to protect from the denizens of some foreign plane, and we don't disappear if we wander outside the circle's boundaries- it is, to quote myself quoting Starhawk, an enacted meditation.

If you believe in the elementals of Paracelsus and John Dee's angels and can reconcile those things with Wicca (I, personally, cannot, as they both require a Christian understanding of the world that I, as a never-been-Christian lack) then they can add powerful things to the circle, but you don't *need* to add to them to give the circle power. The circle has power on its own.

In my case, my training in ceremonial magic left me feeling less like the circle was weak but more like it was not my rite to do. I was trained with an Enacting the Temple Rite that was practically verbatim from Uncle Bucky's Big Blue Book (The Complete Book of Witchcraft by Raymond Buckland.) Those familiar with the rite tend to admit it is a little clunky, but in a Volvo or Volkswagen sort of way…it's not pretty, but it will go 400,000 miles before it really breaks down. It was only as a high priestess, when I started to find myself asked to do more rituals at the intimate level that my discomfort with the rite as written, including as written by my own hand, began to overwhelm the efficacy of the rite enough to require a massive rewrite of what I already had.

I had been thinking about the notions of the family for several years. I feel closer to my ancient ancestors (the Campbells that stole cattle from the ancestors of at least two of the Triad's ancestors, for example) a distant relation in UK and practitioner of magic in her own right told me she was having great success inviting her totemic animal spirits into her workings. Her animals were not from ancient indigenous peoples, but her family's coat of arms.

With her assistance, I explored the meaning of my family heraldric animals, the white boar of Campbell, the Sable Griffon of Morgan and the Salamander of Douglas. It was, in fact, the experiences I would have contacting these beings (which are sort of a cross between ancestors and animals) that would lead to the addition of the Douglas to my last name, not just a simple of acceptance of my place as Phoenix's life mate, but an agreement to submit myself to the will of the Douglas totemic spirit. Anyone who knows the history of the illustrious Campbells knows the Douglases are genetic relations anyways, but this was more.

My ancestors, cousins, grandfathers, and others fought and died under these banners and in the names of these names. (My own pen name, MacMorgan, is a combination of Morgan and Campbell, even if you'll have to trust me on the Campbell part, which is not readily apparent to all but the family historians.) Ceremonial magic has a saying- split blood brings power. A lot of them have misinterpreted this to mean that sacrifice is called for, but what it means is that the idea of Campbell, the idea of Morgan and the idea of Douglas have power- people have been killed and killed others for the meaning of those names.

To harness the power of these names I would undertake a quasi-shamanic journey inappropriate for discussion herein. In doing so, I would discover a forth spirit that guided me, despite my wishes otherwise. My father's family, who I do not communicate with or even hold in high esteem, had a spirit they'd fought and died under, a spirit I, as a Hellenist as well as a Wiccan found myself drawn to despite the Jingoism surrounding it- the Eagle.

It was the Eagle of Rome and of Greek Zeus, and the Eagle of my father's father, a Normandy vet. It was the Eagle of the hills I grew up loving, the same spirit that would guide me home to New York State after September 11th. She is a sign of Liberty, Freedom and Protection from harm. She is swift to act and unlikely to drop prey that falls into her talons even if it bites her hard, and even though she sometimes does stupid, stupid things rooted in injustice, she flies ever higher (Excelsior!) towards liberty and justice for all (eventually.)

If you roll your eyes at the unbridled patriotism, I felt the same way. America as a Totemic Entity was not something I was prepared to deal with, at least not in the second G. W. Bush administration. Nonetheless, this Eagle spoke to me, as clear as my gods and demanded I acknowledge her.

After my journeys, I found myself confronted with a distinct pattern of entities. There was the Eagle of my birth and my father's father, representing air, the Salamander of Douglas, shown flaming through his armor on their arms, the Campbell White Boar, often too quick to battle and too wild to bear but unstoppably fierce in her earthy protection of her kin, and the contradictory Griffon, the winged lion that metaphysicists called air but not air and earth but not earth. This creature, often shown with fish in one hand and lightning in the other is a creature of the sea trade, associated with ships and protection of the fishing fleet. She, like Morgan, is a thing of the sea.

Finding myself with the elements represented within my own genetic history, within my own family history and the causes those of my own blood have fought and died for, the addition of these animals (who I began to understand as actual, not metaphoric, ancestors) to the circle, especially the Samhain circle that would call upon my ancestors, was not really a question of propriety but of common sense. With the alchemical understanding of these critters the necessity of adding them became not merely common sense but inevitable.

Eagle, in the classical sense of the totem, represents purity and power. It is a creature of air but also lightning, a union of air and fire. It is a sign of strength, incredibly masculine in its use of power but feminine in its manifestation.

It is contrasted with Salamander, which represents fire but also earth. It is not the Salamander of Paracelsus, but the enormous land dragon that lives at the flaming core of the earth and is unharmed by the molten earth. He is a creature of power that is used only rarely. He is slow to act and slow to disengage, the opposite of the swift and occasionally rash Eagle. He loves slowly but forever, and in this Salamander's case, it is entrusted with the literal heart that represents Scotland, one of the lands of my ancestors.

Griffon is closest to the osprey in her aspect as a bird. She is a master of the air and the cliffs, but she dives into the water to find her life. She uses cleverness over sheer power, and is slow to rouse but slow to shake her prey. She is a guardian of shipping and industry, and the coat of arms of the famous Henry Morgan (the guy on the Rum bottle) and the famous J.P. Morgan, industrial baron and stakeholder in the Titanic. She is associated with ships but most famous for ships that sank-Queen Anne's Revenge, Satisfaction and Titanic. She is the sea, but in her modern aspect represents oil and money. She is a fierce mistress, prone to revenge, that men are drawn to without understanding her. She is the search for wisdom and the knowledge that no mortal can have it all.

The White Boar of Campbell was the hardest one for me to reconcile with, even though it was the one my students and friend say in me the most. She is vicious and loyal, territorial (including other people's territory, I'm afraid) and ruthless. At the same time she is fecund and wide reaching. There is at least one Campbell of Scottish Campbell descent on six of the seven continents, and sometimes all seven of them. The Boar represents the earth and the unseen, but she's visible and exotic, standing out in the forest just because she breeds so efficiently that if you kill one of her children ten more rise up in her place. In times of threat and war she breeds even more profusely, and her children can often be found on both sides of the conflict, so she fights herself as well.

I found balancing these four aspects in the circle helped me balance them in myself, and as my circle became more an extension of myself and my existence through time than a place beyond place and a time beyond time. I found it got leaner, tighter, more efficient. It felt more like a metaphysical circle of protection than a Wiccan circle, a circle used to keep things in, or out.

This circle could not be broken, or pierced to let energy through, so it was time for another alteration in my personal space... From UEWiccan, May 2008.

....this second rite would become the Compass Rose, perhaps the highlight of the MacMorgan Covenstead sept of CUEW, but the Heraldric circle itself still proved useful for uniting the various entities our ancestors worked with on a constant basis. Although I know this rite will matter little to those outside our genetic families, it's my sincere hope that the material will provide inspiration in how to construct a completely personal rite.

The assembly takes their places around the circle. They stand in a circle within a circle, the radius of the smaller no less than 2/3 that of the larger. Four smaller circles are inscribed, each with a small column within it.

High Priestess stands at east, with a flame kindled from the sun. She says: "East, place of beginnings, to you we turn to begin all things. May we be unfettered and unchained like the winds we represent you with. Fly, oh Eagle of Zeus, symbol of warriors and liberty. Go, that our words be carried to the heights!"

Sacred herbs, laurel, labdanum resin, heather and dragon's blood are thrown upon the coals. The tripod is carried around the circle and all are invited to lustrate. High Priestess walks once inside, once outside and once inside again. As the coals return to the east, she cries: "Eagle of this land, salve! Protect all who gather within from those that would do us harm."

There is a flash from the station of the South as firepowder is added to the coals that sit there. The words almost overlap as the priestess says. "Salamander of the south, shield-borne creature and protector of the clans"—it is acceptable for this to be interrupted by a war cry—"Tester of pride, tempter to virtue, temperer of emotion and will. May we know fire that we know our limits and our strengths, Over-watcher of the just deaths of the unrighteous and unjust deaths of their opposites, hear now our rites tonight!"

Candles are passed around. From the West, the High Priestess speaks as she pours blessed water upon the coals, billowing steam. "I am become the west. Sacred waters that wash away all that is wicked, all evil, all that is unclean. Wrong do-ers tremble at my name. I am Atlantic, Pacific, I am Erie and mighty Niagara[73].

She walks around the circle with a bowl of the blessed water. All touch it and rinse their hands in it. "Touch the water that you never know thirst."

She goes around the outside of the circle, giving the water to the earth. "Water to the earth that the bounty be shared." She circles inside, and at west says "Let the mighty Griffon, fish in his right, sword in his left, guard this rite![74]"

"Strength, flexibility and the ability to cope with change, The Griffon guards its kin."

The remainder of the water is poured upon the flames.

Priestess, from the North: "From the North were we birthed, formed in ice and steel. From the forests and mountains to the vast plains of the diaspora, the clan of the white boar, often hated, often victorious. She roots the ground for sustenance, guards her young with fierceness. Smites the enemies with determination and is ever prepared for the year to come. She is the abiding earth, base of all that nurtures. Touch her and be blessed, feel her and be one."

The purified earth is walked around the circle three times. When it is returned to its place, a handful is tossed upon the fire."

High Priestess, at east. "Now we are one with the elements, protected and guided by the protectors of clan and country. Let none now remain who are unprepared to face the gods of this assemblies' members."

---

[73] Understand this rite generally occurs less than 1/2 of a mile from the meeting of this lake and river.

[74] It is not uncommon for the scions of my family to toast "Fish, Tin and Copper" at this. Remember this is a diaspora rite for Welsh, Cornish and Scottish families, after all.

"Into this circle we call the true gods of our ancestors. Come if you will [Omited,] Come if you will [Omited,] come if you will oh unseen one who greets many. Come all and observe our celebration tonight."

Priestess: "Let this Temple represent a place beyond place, a world beyond worlds, a church without walls and a space without space, for our rites reach into the mind of all-that-is and share it to its core. Let nothing faithless stand within![75]"

High Priestess: "All who are here and all who hear we bade you silence. The rites within are for you, the gods and no others. Let those who lack discretion flee!"

Priestess: "Now is our temple one, and we are one with the temple."

All: "So mote it be!"

---

[75] This is a ritualized brag. If you are unfamiliar with the concept, it may sound hubristic, but it's not. I fully believe the gods understand subtlety!

Afterword: I know how to do this, now what?

Most people who read this work will already know enough about Wicca to not need any help beyond what this book recommends. There will be a few, however, who somehow got this book as a first book on Wicca, or as their first *serious* book on Wicca, and are now wondering what comes next in their ritual practice. This afterword is for them.

Wicca is not exactly renowned for its quality control. There are people who make stuff up, slap the word Wicca on it and sell it at a profit. Most of the best authors about Wicca are people you haven't heard of, from publishers you do not know. I strongly suggest that those new to Wicca find a tradition, any tradition, to learn from. Even a bad choice at the beginning can help you make decisions later. *The Witches' Voice*, http://www.witchvox.com is an excellent resource to find traditions.

Wicca for the rest of us, http://wicca.timerift.net, is a good starting point online, as it will systematically dispel many of the myths that new students start with. The data there can certainly help you distinguish between a good tradition and a bad one. If you use that site to sort the real history of Modern Paganism from the nonsense, you'll weed out more than 90% of the traditions who list on Witchvox that are dreadful. If you choose only those who do not charge from the remainder, you'll probably find a great source.

If you can't find a good tradition online, I recommend reading Ronald Hutton's book *The Triumph of the Moon*, and then reading either the books *Wicca* and *Living Wicca* by Scott Cunningham or *Buckland's Complete Book of Witchcraft* by Raymond Buckland. These three books are flawed, but they will provide you with enough information, though imperfect, to practice on your own.

As for my own words, I recommend the very slim, very tiny book *The Ethical Eclectic* for anyone who intends to blend from more than one source. The book is less than 80 pages, and can be read in a single sitting. I wrote it because so many eclectics have asked for such a thing. Also, if you choose the tradition I follow, Universal Eclectic Wicca, then the aforementioned *All One Wicca* is a great introduction, as is the CUEW website, http://www.cuew.org.

Regardless of who you choose to listen to, check sources, read the words of many and above all ask questions. Do not follow any single source merely because you like that source, or their shiny bookcovers. Check sources, read the opposing side and do the research yourself.

The gods gave you a brain. Use it.

Index

Air in the North, 49
Altered states of
   consciousness, 6
Anael (archangel), 16
ancestors, 3, 9, 10, 11, 12, 22,
   23, 24, 25, 33, 36, 37, 41,
   46, 52, 58, 59, 65, 66, 94,
   96, 103, 120, 122, 123, 125
Archangels, 15, 16, 17, 18, 19,
   20, 21
   names of, 16
Blessed Be, 32
Book of Shadows,
   Gardnerian, 1, 20
Cakes and Ale, 1
casting spells, 65
Casting the Circle. *See*
   Erecting the Temple
Ceremonial Magic, 14, 32, 39,
   47, 49, 65, 84, 85, 87, 94,
   119
Charge of The Goddess, 2
Clavicula Salomonis, 1, 4, 18
Closing the Temple, v, 63
Compass Rose, 6, v, 2, 14, 22,
   43, 45, 46, 79, 81, 82, 86,
   94, 96, 97, 123
Co-operative Temple Rite, 61
Coven
   of equals, 61
Dee, John, 1, 13-16, 20
divination, 65
Drawing Down the Moon, 2
dread lords, 65

Drugs (in the Temple), 7
Elementals, 17, 48, 89
Elements, 48, 49
Enochian, 15
Erecting the Temple, 5, 1, 2, 4
   defined, 1
Excalibur, 21
Fire and Water, 21
five critical states, 55
Five Dimensions, The, i, 3, 5
   energetic, i, iii
   energetic, 24
   mental, 3, 24
   physical, 3, 13
   spiritual, 3, 6
   traditional, 4
Fivefold kiss, 32, 72
Formal Group Temple, 56
Formal Pentagram, 55
Formal Temple for Solitary
   Practice, 51
Gabriel (archangel), 16
guestright, 8, 77
Holistic Temple Rites, 5
Holistic, defined, 35
Kelley, Edward, 15
Key of Solomon, The. *See*
   Clavicula Salomonis
King Arthur, 1, 21
land, sea and air, 43
land, sea and sky, 35, 54
LBRP. *See* Lesser Banishing
   Ritual of the Pentagram

Lesser Banishing Ritual of the Pentagram, 14, 20
Location of the Elements, 49
Lucifer
　archangel, 16
mental preparedness, 69
Michael (archangel), 16
Mighty Ones, 21
minimalist temples, 27, 43, 51
Oriphiel (archangel), 16
Paracelsus, 21
patron deity, 56
Perfect Love and Perfect Trust, 7
prayer beads, 45
preparing the way, 2, 3, 24
Prescriptions in the Temple. *See* Drugs
purification techniques, 55, 67, 69
Raphael (archangel), 16
Rite
　defined, 1
Round Table, King Arthur's, 1
Sacrosanct Land, 3
Samael (archangel), 16
Sola Scriptura, 16
Tetragrammaton, 13
totemic spirits, 65
Triarchy of Man, 21, 78
UEW, ii, 3, 22, 24
Visualizations, Elemental (in UEW), 3, 24, 28
Watchers, 48, *See* Watchtowers
Watchtowers, *14*, 19, 20, 33, 48, 49, 87, 92, 93
When to not use the Temple, v, 65
Will, 8
Zachariel (archangel), 16
ἵππος (horses [of Revelation]), 18